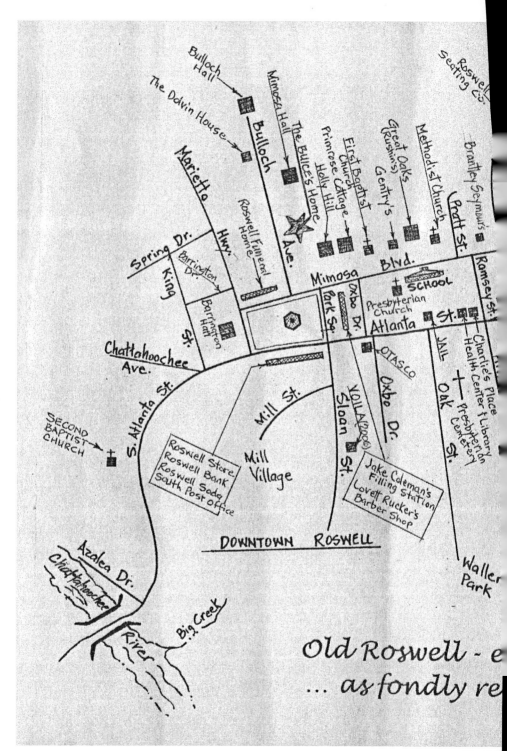

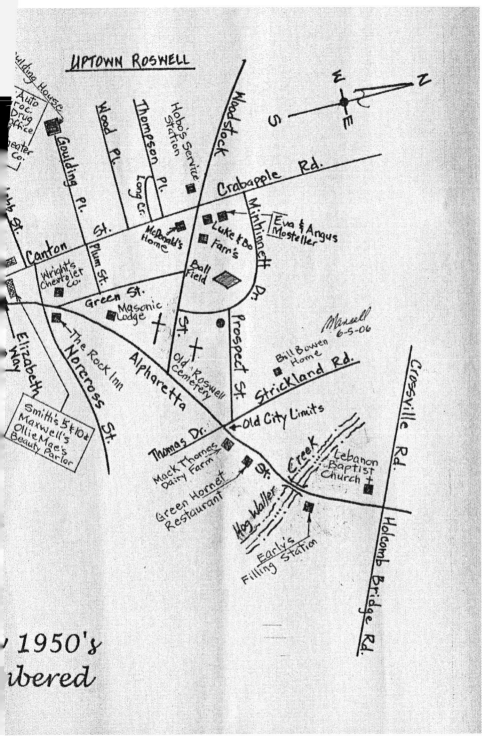

Lela (Bo) Whitener, 1939

Bo Buice, A Woman After God's Own Heart

Linda Mansell Martin

Canton, Georgia

2005-06

Copyright © 2007 by Linda Mansell Martin.

Library of Congress Control Number:		2006909747
ISBN:	Hardcover	978-1-4257-4183-9
	Softcover	978-1-4257-4182-2

All rights reserved. No part of this book may be reproduced or transmitted in any form or by any means, electronic or mechanical, including photocopying, recording, or by any information storage and retrieval system, without permission in writing from the copyright owner.

This book was printed in the United States of America.

To order additional copies of this book, contact:
Xlibris Corporation
1-888-795-4274
www.Xlibris.com
Orders@Xlibris.com
37480

Contents

About the Author ix
Acknowledgments xi
Preface xiii
Foreword xv
Introduction xvii

MORNING

Home and Family 1
The College and Early Teaching Years 13
Bo's Beaus 21
Luke Buice 29
Ervin Luther Buice, I And II 39

NOON

On Ervin and Friendship 53
Jason and MaryEm's Love Song 75
Bo, The School Teacher 87
The Church in the Buice's Life 97
Bo, The Deacon 109
Some of Bo's Teachings 121
Bo's Students Share What She Taught 127
How Others Relate to Bo 135

EVENING

The Departures 153
Growing Old 171

Epilogue 183
Omega 187

Bo Buice (90) & Linda Mansell Martin, (Author) April, 2005

All the darkness in the world cannot put out the light of one small candle.
(unknown)

About the Author

My name is Linda Mansell Martin, and I am a native of Roswell, Georgia, the second largest city in Georgia, and the third best place to raise children according to a recent study. I'm now living in Canton in northwest Georgia, and am a graduate of Trinity University of Deerfield, Illinois with a BS Degree in Communications. In addition, I am a certified Precept Bible Teacher having taught Bible Studies for the past 25 years. I compiled a family cookbook, *"A Measure of Love,"* which has been widely distributed and a Bible Study on Marriage, *"Love Beyond Measure"* which I've also written and taught at several churches.

Alan Martin, also of Roswell, is my husband of 42 years, and we have three fine married sons: Russell Alan, Thomas Anthony (Tony) and Ryan Coleman Martin. We are the proud grandparents of Sheppard, 15; MacKenzie, 10; Aly, 9; Reed, 7; Tucker, 7; Anna, 5; Joshua, 5; and Thomas, 2. Our wonderful daughters-in-law are: Liz, Page and Stephanie.

Jason Byce (Ervin Buice), my good friend, and I shared the same birthday, and we attended kindergarten through 12th grade together. He sang at our wedding. Bo Buice, his mother, was my favorite Sunday School Teacher, at Roswell First Baptist Church, when I was a young mother. She made a lasting impact on my life. As she puts it, "Linda was one of my students who didn't forget me." How could I? My mother died when I was 15, and I needed all the mothering and teaching I could get from older, wiser women. Mrs. Buice happened to be one of my favorites.

Bo, MaryEm and I are all teachers, so we all have "taught" in the following pages. Teachers teach. Sometimes we didn't always agree on everything, but we certainly chose to agree to disagree, but to keep our love flowing. Jesus instructed His followers to "Go ye, therefore, and teach all nations, ... teaching them to observe all things whatsoever I have commanded you; and lo, I am with you always, even unto the end of the world." (Matthew 28:20)

Billy Graham has been known for and has found that "people everywhere, all over the world, respond to the gospel of Jesus Christ if it is presented simply and with Christian compassion." This is what I've tried to do also in these pages.

"It's not about you," is how Rick Warren's book, ***The Purpose Driven Life*** begins. So this book is mostly about God and His purpose and plan for all of us. Yes, Bo, Luke, MaryEm and Ervin (Jason) were the subjects used, but the real story is about Him and His purpose and plan for our individual lives.

The Bible is made up of many true stories, and the lives of many people—people just like you and me. It doesn't hold back on sharing the truth of their lives—the good, the bad and the ugly. In this way, we can identify with those people. Jesus taught in parables—earthly stories with heavenly consequences. I've chosen to do the same—share stories of people's lives so that we can somehow try to identify and hopefully make the right choices. "Choose you this day whom you will serve . . . . but as for me and my house, we will serve the Lord." (Joshua 24:15)

My sister, after reading the book said, "It is wonderful—so interesting." I hope that most of you feel the same.

Linda M. Martin
June 2, 2006
11:00 P.M. —DONE!!

Acknowledgments

B*o Whitener Buice, A Woman After God's Own Heart*, could not have been written without the help, friendship, cooperation and inspiration of so many. Thank you all!

To the Heavenly Father, the Beloved Son, and the Holy Spirit, the Trinity, Who gave me the divine inspiration when I didn't know how or what to write, but Who always came through for me to give me the words and the wisdom I needed.

To Bo Buice, my teacher, friend and mentor, for her inspiration and joy as we spent much time together collecting, remembering, organizing and encouraging each other in the long process of writing, reading, deleting and rewriting her life story as contained in this book.

To MaryEm Byce, Bo's daughter-in-law and my new friend, who "filled in" the missing pieces and labored in rewriting the chapters pertaining to her and Jason.

To my adorable Alan, my husband of 42 years, who patiently put up with my moods and illnesses while I was trying to wade through all the many complications of writing. Thank him for his perseverance in editing the manuscript.

To Jean and Jerry Haymaker, my dear sister and brother-in-law, who helped me also in editing and correcting. As Jean said, "It is more than a biography. You took Bo's life and added all the fluff and pillows and decorations, so that people could identify and use it to apply to their homes and families."

Tim Combs, our friend, fellow author, and fellow Sunday School Class Member, now deceased, who helped me with some details that the men would enjoy.

To Bruce Wilkinson, author of the book, **The Dream Giver**, who inspired me to keep following my dream, when I wanted to give up and quit. He actually taught me the stages to expect and follow to get to the goal! Thanks, indirectly to Dan and Margie Curry, who gave the book to Bo, who passed it on to me to read when I was at my lowest point emotionally.

To my dear friend, Diane Dorris, who was my "shoulder to cry on" when the going got rough. She encouraged me, even when she told me to "put a ribbon on the thing and put it in a drawer," which I did for a day. But then, having "let go," I was able to pull it out again and to finish by the deadline—eighteen months of actual writing and correcting for the "baby" to be born.

To Margaret and Jim Ovbey, good friends of the Buices for many years, who also helped fill in the missing parts of the school teaching years.

To all my new friends in the Bo Buice Sunday School Class at Roswell First Baptist Church for all their help and to Dr. Ron Bradley, my Pastor, for his example of impartiality.

To my fellow classmates from Roswell High School, Class of '62, and their contributions and accolades because they loved Ervin and his parents also.

To Brenda Bowen Mansell for the map and to my daughter-in-law, Liz, for the graphic cover art work. Thanks!!

Bo would like to thank everyone who had any part in her life story! She loves you all! She also wants you to know that she loves all Christians—not just Baptists!! In fact, she loves everyone just as Jesus does.

Bo & I would like to thank the wonderful people at Xlibris who have been so helpful in the publication process!

Preface

Many people begin well on life's road, when they are young and strong with hopes and dreams—but many detach or drop out, when the storms come and the trials and stresses cause them to become bitter, antisocial, reclusive or simply uncaring and unfriendly—but Bo Buice of Roswell, Georgia has a wonderful track record, going strong at 91 years of age. She is friend, teacher, mentor and spiritual mother to many, including me. Her story is one that will hopefully inspire and encourage you to go the distance and to finish well. Her teachings and inspirational gems are embedded within the stories.

My prayer is that you will find encouragement to endure and to make an impact in your generation for good as I believe Bo Whitener Buice has in her's.

Linda M. Martin

> *"'Faith grows amid storms'.... So in the spiritual world, when you see a giant, remember the road he or she has traveled has not always been along a sunny lane where wildflowers bloom, but a steep, rocky, narrow pathway, where the blasts of hell will almost blow you off your feet.... It is a pathway of sorrow and joy, of suffering and healing balm, of tears and smiles, of trials and victories, of conflicts and triumphs, of hardships and perils and buffetings, of persecutions and misunderstandings, of troubles and distress; through all of which we are made more than conquerors through Him who loves us."* —E. A. Kilbourne

Warning: This story of one woman's life-changing journey could change your life!

Foreword

In the giddy bustle of modern life, there are few persons that exert a life-long imprint on human lives more than parents, a particular minister, or a special classroom teacher. Author, Linda M. Martin, in artistic strokes has directed our attention to Bo (Lela) Buice, a brilliant Baptist teacher and heroine, who early in life rejected brashness, class warfare, and incivility, to achieve remarkable social progress in the public solidity, her quiet persuasiveness, and all-embracing Christian love. As Linda expertly reveals, Bo Buice is attended by a rainbow of optimism, wit, compassion and success.

Committed first to her Lord, secondly, to her church, thirdly, to research and the study of history and finally, to civic activities, this exceptional lady, at age 91, continues to be the image of grace, charity and beauty.

—D. Lawrence H. Harris,
Author of The Origins and Growth of Baptist Faith:
Twenty Baptist Trailblazers in World History.

Introduction

Early in 2005, I was inspired to write Bo's story and I approached her with my idea. She was elated!! She said that it gave her a reason to keep living after all the losses in her life. She said she felt close to me, and that when I entered the room, it was as if her son entered with me. (Bo has a way of making everyone feel loved and appreciated) So, in June, 2005 we began our journey of putting together the many pieces of the puzzle of her fascinating story.

In November, Bo and I traveled together via AmTrak to visit her lifelong friend, Nelle Hayes Arden, 89, in Fairfax, Virginia. We had a wonderful adventure, and I loved getting to see the two of them reunite face to face after a 20-year lapse of time (see photograph) even though they talk every week by telephone. On Wednesday of the week we were there, Bo proclaimed, "Let's go to Washington!" Since we were only a few miles away, and since Nelle had a car, I said, "Okay, let's go." (Inside I was thinking, "I can do all things through Christ who gives me the strength." I can't do this in my own strength—only through His.) Nelle had not been into the city for 12 years, and at the last minute, decided to go with us. Later she said how much she also enjoyed our wonderful day.

The day was glorious when we toured our Nation's Capitol, even though the weathermen had predicted stormy weather. The leaves were a glorious array of fall colors, the temperature was cool, but sunny. I felt Ervin's spirit with me that day, and of course, the Holy Spirit, giving me supernatural strength and stamina. We visited the World War II Memorial, since both Nelle and Bo's husbands were involved in that war. Then we visited the Korean Memorial. By the time we found the Vietnam Memorial, Bo was getting weary, so I obtained a wheelchair and wheeled her to the place where we stood by all the names of those who gave their lives for our freedom.

In addition, we saw the Washington Monument, the Lincoln Memorial, the Jefferson Memorial, the White House, the Capitol and Arlington Cemetery. We were inspired by the words, "Freedom is not free," and by the inscription that America does not come to put people in bondage but to set them free from tyranny. Oh, what a glorious day we had. An oriental man took our picture as I was wheeling Bo around. We laughed and enjoyed the beauty all around us that day—and surprisingly there was very little traffic. I think many believed that a storm was coming and avoided the city that day. We know that God parted the clouds just for us.

When we were about to board the train in Alexandria, Virginia after dark for our return trip to Atlanta, the steward carted us out to a little waiting station for the handicapped passengers. There was a large black man standing by Bo who was not handicapped, so we didn't realize until later why he was there. When the train arrived, I left her for a minute to put our luggage on the train, and as I turned around, I saw Bo and this man fall headfirst on the concrete!! Actually, he broke her fall but went down with her. He was an angel, we're convinced, as we never saw him again, and Bo was totally unharmed. I was, however, shaken severely, but grateful for the divine intervention.

On our return trip, our train hit a car in Buford, Georgia, just 20 minutes from the Peachtree Street Station, and we were stranded for three hours. The man in the car was killed, who disregarded the signals, and the lowered railroad crossing arms. This reminded me of how many people today are ignoring the signs all around them which indicate that something is seriously wrong, that we need to dust off and return to the Instruction Manual on Living and obey what the Owner's Manual teaches. We need to pay attention to the warning signals and the boundaries established by God for our good and His glory. We also need to slow down and take time to be still and get to know God. He has left us with plenty of evidence.

Bo and I used those three hours to work on more of this book, so for us the time was not wasted. We were prepared to keep remembering and recording. Others on the train weren't so prepared. They were just murmuring and complaining.

It is Springtime now, sitting by my window with the rain pitter-pattering outside, as I write and rewrite this story. I had a dream the other night which caused me to awaken suddenly and tearfully. I was experiencing the heart of God as He must be saddened by the hurts and pains of His creation, with wars, destruction, displaced and fragmented families, crime and violence, sin and suicides, broken hearts and homes, stressed out people trying to gain more and more money, only to find themselves hopelessly unhappy and unfulfilled. The prayer needs grow greater and deeper the older I get, and the more I experience. I awakened heart-broken for our land, our world, our homes, our families, our

INTRODUCTION

sick. But there is a Light in the darkness. His light always shines brightest when the darkness is threatening to engulf us. Run to the Lighthouse.

I read a devotional recently in II Chronicles 1, where Solomon asked God for wisdom when God asked him, "What should I give you?" God answered him, "Because you have not requested riches, wealth, or glory, nor for the lives of those who hate you, and you have not even asked for long life, but you have asked for wisdom and knowledge that you may judge My people over whom I have made you king, wisdom and knowledge are given you; I will also give you riches, wealth and glory . . . ." As I read this, I asked God for wisdom on how to write and publish this book. I didn't ask for glory, nor wealth nor fame. I just asked for wisdom, and I believe that He has honored that prayer as I really didn't know how to write it.

Then, on vacation, I found this quote from Mother Teresa, "We are all pencils in the hand of God." Well, that was all the encouragement I needed to finish what I had begun.

It is my prayer that as you read these pages about one godly woman, her life and her family, I pray that you will be inspired to persevere, to love your God, and your family deeper, to not give up nor drop out when the road becomes long and difficult. This woman has weathered many a storm, and has touched thousands of lives. She's a living inspiration. Her smile and humor is contagious, her faith catching, her joy radiant, her love sincere. She will make you smile and make you cry. She will hold you in suspense, and teach you things you didn't know. She will inspire you not to give up when life throws you a curve or pulls the rug out from beneath your feet. I hope that this story of one woman's journey through the ups and downs of life will leave you a better person when you get to the end of the story. I pray that you won't compare yourself to her but to Christ, who makes each of us unique as the snowflakes, but that you will be encouraged to follow the Savior, when you read this endearing story of one woman's faithful journey. I hope that you will decide to follow the Lord, and study His Words in the Book which the Holy Spirit inspired to teach us how to live and to "THINK," as Bo loves to say. In truth, this book, hopefully, will cause you to think.

In the Saturday, Sunday Edition of The Wall Street Journal, dated May 6,7, 2006, there is a story about a woman named Virginia Lawson, age 96, who lives in Southampton, N.Y. alone in her home. Her only son, Evan, a lawyer, lives in Boston. The story was about how she shoveled the snow, saying, "Someone might come." But no one came. She gets one phone call a day, from an agency checking on her status. The sad part to me were two sentences which she was quoted as saying. "Since she says she has no use for religion, there is no church to attend." (And no church to attend to her!) And the second was, "I don't need people. I can build my own world." Well, Bo Buice, at 91, thinks exactly opposite. She would not have survived without her church and friends, wonderful people who have reciprocated the love which she poured into them, who are now pouring it back to her!! I believe this is the way God intended people to live. People need God and people need other people!

Lest I give you the impression that Bo and Luke Buice were perfect people and had a perfect life, let me assure you as author Elizabeth Elliott once said, "There are no perfect families. We are all dysfunctional to some extent because we live in an imperfect world." Someday the Perfect will come, but until then, we're waiting and seeking excellence in our own selves and the people we uphold as role models.

This book is dedicated to Madeline (you will find who she was as you read) and all the younger ones in our families, both Bo's and mine, that they will not forget . . . . "for those who do not learn from history are destined to repeat it." Remember: History is His Story. This is Bo's story inspired by God's hand on her life and mine and the other family members.

Blessings,
For the glory of God,

Linda Mansell Martin
Mother's Day Week, 2006

AGE

Age is Life's recorded Message
Of our minutes, days and years.
Hopeful morning, busy noon-time,
Evening, hinting rest is near.

In our *morning*, hope inspires us;
By ambitious youth we're led
Ever strong and striving onward,
Eager for each task ahead.

Age at *noon-time* will remind us
We have traveled half the race;
Social climbing, job declining . . . .
Friends and children join the pace.

Evening comes, and now our message
Shows the value of design.
God's own hand and good, unmeasured
Guide this life to One Divine.

—Bo Buice
(National Library of Congress—Famous
Poets of America, 2003)

This will Certify that

Bo Buice

is a member in good standing

International Society of Poets
1995-1996

and is recognized for support of
The Society's principles of
Peace - Education - Accomplishment
Charity - Equality

Elizabeth Barnes
Elizabeth Barnes
President

International Society of Poets Award

The National Library of Poetry

11419-10 Cronridge Drive • Post Office Box 704 • Owings Mills, Maryland 21117 • (410) 356-2000

Bo Buice
83 Bulloch Ave
Roswell GA 30075

Dear Bo,

Thank you for your entry in our recent contest. Your poem was recognized by the judges as being among the best 3% of all entries judged. We are therefore pleased to award you our Editor's Choice Award for your contest entry as published in *A Delicate Balance*. Congratulations on your significant achievement.

Sincerely,

The National Library of Poetry

Editor's Choice Award

Presented to

Bo Buice

for Outstanding Achievement in Poetry
Presented By
The National Library of Poetry
1995

Cynthia Stevens
Editor

Caroline Sullivan
Editor

National Library of Poetry Award

MORNING

Bo's Mother, Lela White's Family: Bo's Grandfather, John S. White, seated; son (left), Hass; daughter, Isabelle, (died young); Lela (Bo's mother) & son, George. (another son, Jim, not shown). Approximately 1902, when their mother died.

Clarice (Cat) 3, & Lela (Bo) 2, 1917

Home and Family

On a sunny, warm day in April, the 28th to be exact, in the year of our Lord, 1915, a beautiful blonde baby girl was born at home to Lela Mae and Horace Cleveland (Cleve) Whitener in Chattanooga, Tennessee. Lela named this second daughter after herself, but when little Lela was still quite young, the minister who had married her parents, started calling little Lela "little Bo Peep," which name endured until she was about eight and her mother said no more "little" or "peep," giving Bo Whitener her nickname for life, a name which fits her perfectly, as Bo has spent a lifetime collecting her own "sheep," people who would also follow the Good Shepherd.

Lela White, Bo's mother, born in 1890, was reared near Chickamauga, Tennessee. Unfortunately, her mother died when Lela was twelve, and she had to assume responsibility for the care of her two younger brothers, George and Haas. Her sister, Isabelle, also died young. Lela stood on a box to cook for the family. She managed to go to school, and eventually became a teacher in a one-room schoolhouse. Very refined, with high ideals, Bo's mother was patient, kind and gifted. Lela and Horace Cleveland Whitener were married on December 24, 1911 in Chattanooga. Cleve and Lela were blessed with three children, and Lela stayed home to love and train them: Clarice, Lela (Bo) and Horace Cleve, named for his father. Lela cooked delicious meals, made clothes for her children, spent quality and quantity time with each of them, often taking them to the library and to Sunbeams at Church.

Horace Cleveland Whitener (Cleve), Bo's father, was born on September 28, 1886 to William E. and Augusta Nichols Whitener of Dalton, Georgia. The fourth of ten children born to farm parents, in Whitfield County, Cleve was reared in the Mt. Home area, near Dalton, and his formal education ended at a one-room school. His siblings were: Henry, Willie (who married Catherine, "The

Chenille Lady"—see photo), Roy, John, Tom (Susan's Dad, see photos at end of book), Belle, Annie Mae, Gertrude, and Ed, who died at 21 from diabetes.

Cleve left home to find work in a store in Dalton and later was a piano and organ salesman, having learned to play the piano well, and led music in evangelistic services. He was quite handsome, warm, friendly, and outgoing. He was basically self-taught, and became quite a successful Pastor, Leader and Father.

Following Cleve and Lela's marriage in 1911, and the birth of Clarice in 1913, and Bo in 1915, Cleve was called into the ministry at age 27, and received the invitation to serve the Mt. Home Baptist Church in Morganton, North Carolina. (Some of the pioneer Whitener's are buried near Morganton.) He became a very popular Baptist minister due to his outgoing personality and friendly, robust laughter. In going through some of her father's papers, Bo and I were astonished at the manner in which her father was often paid—in vegetables and even once an opossum! Her father was not only the Preacher, but he was also the choir director and the pianist and was paid by chickens!

In Morganton, when Bo was about four, she got in trouble while her father was preaching. She and her mother and sister were sitting on the front pew of the church and Bo got up and started running around, for which she later received a good spanking from her father. She never ran around in church after that—maybe in other places, but never in church. Spankings do have a lasting effect on young children as the scriptures dictate. "Do not withhold discipline from a child; if you spank them, they won't die. If you spank them, you will save them from death." (Proverbs 23:13-14)

While Bo was five years old, Rev. Whitener was called to the Highland Baptist Church in Hickory, North Carolina. The family moved into a small house until the pastorium could be built. Bo recalls riding in their one-seated "Huppmobile," an auto made between 1909 and 1940 in the workingman's price range, with Clarice sitting in the middle and Bo on her mother's lap, while holding their cat, named Tabby.

Fearfully, Bo started to school in Hickory, and she cried the first day. When her parents came for her, she told them a lie, saying Mr. Barb, the Principal, stepped on her foot. She soon adjusted and loved school and her first grade teacher, Miss Hollingsworth, and her friends, Rachael Fox and Josephine Hyder.

Bo was ten years of age when she accepted Christ in a revival service at Highland Baptist Church. While the congregation sang, "Just As I Am," on the second verse, Bo heard, "Just as I am and waiting not," she got up and went to the altar to make a public profession of her faith. Rev. and Mrs. Whitener were happy at that moment to see their little girl give her life to the Lord Jesus at such an early age, remembering the words of the Jesus who said, "Allow the children

HOME AND FAMILY

to come unto Me and do not forbid them, for of such belongs the kingdom of God." (Matthew 19:14)

Bo was eight and Clarice was ten, living in Hickory when their baby brother, Horace Cleveland Whitener, Jr. was born. While playing in sandbox with her two-year-old baby brother the day after her conversion, Bo thanked God for her salvation and for her little brother. Her prayer life had already begun at this young age. God loves the attitude of gratitude in His people. Life was good.

But then tragedy struck. Sometimes when we least expect it, something happens to test our faith in God. Bo was ten and Clarice was twelve at the time. Rev. Whitener had taken both his daughters with him on a church-related visit, while Mrs. Whitener was visiting her father who was ill in Tennessee. Bo was sitting in the front seat of their car with her father and Clarice was in the back seat, when a bullet came through the canvas top and struck Clarice in the back of her head! Rev. Whitener rushed her to the hospital and left Bo in the car for hours while Clarice was having an operation to remove the bullet and a portion of her brain. Only part of the bullet could be removed due to severe bleeding. Meanwhile Bo was hungry, frightened and needing her mother and a bathroom. What a test for such young girls and Rev. Whitener. There were no cell phones in those days! But God was with them. His line is always open: "Call on Me and I will show you great and mighty things that you do not know. (Jeremiah 33:3) Cleve and Bo called and God answered affirmatively. Clarice's life and mind were spared!

The police never discovered who fired the shot, but they suspected it may have come from a disgruntled person who had heard Rev. Whitener's previous sermon on the ills of alcohol.

Bo, always thinking the best, believes until this day, the incident was an accident. The only lasting effect on Clarice was a vision problem the rest of her life. Mentally, she never suffered and eventually became the Valedictorian and Honor Graduate of her high school class of 1931.

In 1926, Pastor Cleve Whitener, Bo's father, and the family moved to Georgia, where he was called to serve The First Baptist Church at Buford. There he served for the next 19 years. The family lived in the pastorium while there.

Rev. Whitener spearheaded the erection of a new Sanctuary and Educational building, totally debt free which was unheard of in those days. His pastorate there was generally regarded as one of the most successful among Southern Baptists. In Buford, he had the first standard Sunday School in the state. It was January 15, 1933, during the height of the Depression, when the Sunday School annex was dedicated and on that day the last dollar was contributed. In an article, dated January 12, the following words from the Christian Index explains the significance of this feat:

"Pastor Whitener and his loyal people have shown the way to high achievement in the Depression. One of the first things placed on his proposed program was a modern Sunday School plant. They paid as they built, and on the day of dedication, the last dollar was contributed."

From an article in the Atlanta Journal, dated June 20, 1941, the journalist told how the congregation had built their new sanctuary under the direction of Rev. Whitener:

"The spark of vision started way back in 1925, when John D. Carter, a member of the Board of Deacons, deposited a small sum of money in the bank and said it was to be the beginning of a new church. How or by whom it was to be built remained to be seen. All during the year, the fund grew. Not by leaps and bounds, but at a pace that never slackened until the job was completed **fifteen years later**. The widow's mite and the merchant's dollar, the baby's bank penny and the housewives' egg money all went into the building fund."

In 1945, Horace Cleveland (Cleve) Whitener, became Secretary of the Department of Evangelism for the Georgia Baptist Convention, and the family moved to Brookhaven after serving the Buford First Baptist. He served several terms on the Executive Committee of the Convention and also on the Georgia Baptist Hospital Commission.

By 1952, Mercer University conferred the Honorary Doctor of Divinity Degree on Dr. Whitener in recognition of his contribution to the Baptist Denomination. He retired January 1, 1955, after serving ten years in the Evangelism Department.

—

When the Whitener family moved to Buford in January of 1926, and final exam time came in the spring, the tests covered the entire year's material and for which the two girls were unfamiliar. Both Bo and Clarice (Cat—Bo's nickname for her because as a child she couldn't pronounce "Clarice"), failed their exams. This was unlike them, and the teachers advised the Whitener's to hold them back and repeat their grades. This decision proved to benefit both girls. Better to be ahead scholastically rather than behind, the Whitener's reasoned.

In Buford, Bo owned her first bicycle and skates. She enjoyed playing on two long, hilly sidewalks in front of their home. Skinning her knees and chin didn't stop Bo from the fun she had playing after school with her friends and siblings. "For a just man (or woman) falls seven times and rises up again." (Proverbs 24:16a) Falling and getting hurt are all part of the growing up process. From these experiences, children learn caution.

At Buford High School, Bo played basketball, and in one game against Cumming High, she made 13 points of the winning score. She was also on the debate team for two years, and won the honor of going to state competition in essay writing. Balancing academic and extra-curricular activities helped her to be "well-rounded" and taught her the team concept, of working together with others.

In high school, Bo had numerous friends, but her closest girlfriends were Nelle Hayes and Mildred Beard. Nelle and Bo first met at Buford Elementary School when they were eleven years old, and they have remained lifelong friends. They've talked and shared secrets, sorrows and joyous times through the years. "There is a friend who sticks closer than a brother," (Proverbs 18:24), the scripture tells us, and Nelle's friendship has certainly been that kind for Bo. They shared clothes, visits, fond memories, and enjoyed attending G.A.'s (Girls' Auxiliary) together at Buford Baptist Church.

When Bo graduated from Buford High School in 1933, Rev. Whitener gave the Invocation, and had been so busy with his church building program, he was surprised when his youngest daughter, Bo, rose to give the Honor's Speech. He should have known that Clarice had given one at her graduation two years prior and that Bo wouldn't want her sister to out shine her! Wasn't she gifted with speaking and writing, which she had inherited from her father, along with his wonderful sense of humor? We can imagine how he felt that day, hearing his daughter's speech and thanking God for His goodness and mercy to the Whitener family!

Dr. Adrian Rogers, Pastor of the Belview Baptist Church of Memphis, Tennessee, now deceased, is credited with having said, "It takes a family—to raise a child. Home is the only part of Eden we have left." Children thrive in a home where there is love, order and where people love God and each other and assume their roles as God has ordained in His Word.

This chapter of Bo Whitener's life was over but another was soon on the horizon, at her acceptance to the University of Georgia to begin in the Fall of that year. The Whitener children were sent to college and didn't lack for anything. This is quite a testimony to God's provision on behalf of His children. "Yet I've never seen the righteous forsaken and His seed begging bread," (Psalm 37:25b) was certainly true for the Whitener's during those early, struggling years which most young couples face. The struggle is actually good for them—it helps them to bond and pull together, and they become strong through every "storm" they face together and overcome with God's enablement.

Bo believes her parents' success in rearing three God-honoring children, was due in part to her parents' being equally-yoked in Christ, loving each other, and cherishing their children. They taught them by example and the children gradually "caught" their parents' faith over a long period of time. Her mother stayed home to rear the three children. Although a teacher herself, she made this decision, since her own mother had died when she was young and she understood the importance of a mother's presence in the home. Someone has said, "We teach the children loud and clear—what they see is what they hear!" Clarice, Bo and Horace had a wonderful legacy of godliness passed down to them by their parents. They weren't abandoned for the sake of ministry and making money, nor were they neglected for the same pursuits. Rev. Whitener loved the ministry, but he loved God and his family more!

Proverbs 22:6 teaches us to "Train up a child in the way he should go, (according to his bent), and when he is old he will not depart from it." Teaching and training are both taught and caught. Both teaching and training takes much time and effort on the part of parents. If either is neglected, and the children are left to themselves to learn, or if they are taught the wrong things, they suffer as a result. We parents have a very short window of opportunity to have a good influence on the lives of our children. Children need parents who are present more than presents!! Rev. Whitener taught his children to tithe from the time they were small by dividing his tithe between the three of them to put in the offering plate each Sunday. Bo has continued this discipline throughout her life.

Children are our greatest natural resource!

God's Word is His handbook on Life, His love letter to His people containing instructions on how to live, how to raise our children, and how to have successful homes, families and churches. We all need to "get back to the Book." Children need parents who are there and who care, love, hug, discipline and encourage them daily, as Bo's parents were.

If you weren't as fortunate as Bo to be reared in a warm, Christian, happy, secure home, don't get discouraged. God has a way of "working all things together for good to those who love Him and who are called to do His purpose." (Romans 8:28)

"Though no one can go back and make a brand new start, anyone can start now and make a brand new ending!" (Carl Bard)

Bo Buice as a 3rd Grader—Hickory, N.C.

The Buford Baptist Church, Buford, Georgia where Bo's Father, H.C. Whitener pastored for 18 years- 1926-1944

The Whitener Family Home—Pastorium—during their time in Buford, Georgia

Bo Whitener as a teenager

Bo's Family of Origin: Horace, Jr., Clarice (Cat), Bo, Lela (mother) & Horace Cleveland (Cleve) Whitener

Bo's mother: Lela Mae Whitener

Lela (Bo) Whitener in her Graduation Gown—1937

The College and Early Teaching Years

Lela Mae (Bo) Whitener entered the University of Georgia in the fall of 1933. At that time, the coordinate campus was separate from the main university campus, and students would stand on the street corners and the towns' people would stop and "pick them up" and take them to class, which is, of course, unheard of today, 73 years later. Bo took some classes at the coordinate campus, and some at the main campus. She majored in Social Studies and minored in English.

Nelle Hayes, her good friend from elementary and high school, was her roommate in Broadwell Hall Bo's freshman and half of her sophomore year. They enjoyed eating junk food at Cody David's Drug Store in Athens, when they both attended UGA. Bo was on the coordinate campus until she was able to move into the sorority house, but Nelle was her roommate the first year, until she had to drop out for a year. Nelle remembers one Philosophy Class which she and Bo had together and an exam which they both finished simultaneously. When they took their exams to Dr. Wrighton's desk, he asked, "How did the two of you synchronize?" to which Nelle exclaimed, "I don't know." They thought he thought they had cheated, but that was not the case at all—they weren't sure what he was implying. Both girls were good students and it was just an unusual coincidence.

Nelle's family of four sisters and one brother, and her parents, Mr. and Mrs. Penley Hayes, moved to Athens, and she remembers that her Dad paid $40 per month for the rent on their house on Oglethorpe Street. Her father was a rural letter carrier in 1933 when Roosevelt was President, when she returned to college and met her future husband, Louis Arden, a handsome, young Jewish man. They married five years later, and Nelle and Lou had two sons, Alan and Stephen, and now have four grandchildren and two great grandchildren. Louis died in 1993, leaving Nelle. She now lives in an assisted living Fairfax, Virginia in an assisted living home. She and Bo talk every week. She is Bo's oldest living friend, at 89. (See the introduction of our trip to visit Nelle in November of 2005). As of the writing of this book, Mary Grace Wages, Nelle and Bo are the only people still living from their high school graduation class from Buford unless maybe David Mason, Nelle added.

The second half of her sophomore year, Bo moved into the Alpha Gamma Delta Sorority House on Prince Avenue in Athens. There she made some new friends, including her house mother, Sue. Bo is still shocked that her parents allowed her to live in the sorority house. Back then the rules were more strict than they are in today's lenient society where many of the dorms are co-ed. The young women were expected to show courtesy and good manners, and to act in a refined way, especially at mealtime.

In those days the Home, Church, Schools and College all taught basically the same things and were in unity. Unfortunately, that has all changed, and today the disunity in these God-ordained institutions causes young people much confusion as they attempt to find their identity and the purpose for which they are to live. Freedom of speech has come to mean "freedom to explore all options," and "Values Clarification" teaches that values are "relative to the moment." Einstein said that relativity only applied to physics not to human values. All people, including the young, still need rules. Training takes time and much discipline.

The training and learning that Bo got while attending the University of Georgia, as well as her stable home and church life, all contributed to developing exceptional personal relationship skills, which she still utilizes today in a very effective way. She is tactful, kind and friendly with everyone.

Bo attended the First Baptist Church of Athens where Dr. Jim Wilkinson, a good friend of Bo's father, was Pastor. She loved the Sunday School Class for students, and also joined the Baptist Student Union (BSU) at UGA. In 1939, while serving as Corresponding Secretary for the state Baptist Student Union, Bo visited other churches within the association and gave the following speeches:

"For Me to Live is Christ," at Prince Avenue in Athens; "Christ, My Partner for an Abundant Life," in Thomaston, Georgia; "Christ, Lord of My Life" at the BSU Convention in in Gainesville, Florida; "Faith," in Washington, Georgia and "Let Your Light Shine" in Montezuma, Georgia.

Bo's father received a letter from one of his close friends, Walter Adams after Bo had spoken at his church, teasingly congratulating **her mother** for having such a gifted daughter. The letter was dated March 31, 1936 from Pastor Adams at the Madison Baptist Church. (See the attached letter)

Following college graduation from the University of Georgia in 1937, Bo was selected to teach at Duluth High School where she taught for the next two

THE COLLEGE AND EARLY TEACHING YEARS

years. Many of her students were almost her own age. There were four boys in her class and eight or nine girls. Bo taught juniors and seniors Social Studies and English. To her surprise, she had to teach a course in Economics, a course for which she had very little training in college. She really had to study to teach this course. She commented, "I loved it, however." Bo was so young herself but she definitely found her "calling"—teaching, which she loved.

In the 1990's, Bo heard from one of her male students, Marion Corley, from Duluth, who tracked her down by phone, saying, "Mrs. Buice, do you remember me? You taught me at Duluth High School." He would call her periodically, and Bo always wanted to meet him personally, but that never happened because he died with a stroke before they could be reunited—but hopefully one day in heaven they'll be reunited, as with all others whose lives she's touched who have preceded her there! (See photo of this class)

Bo's father took her back and forth to her job in Duluth for several months until she got a room in the home of the fine Sommerville family where she roomed with another teacher, Nelle Cobb. Nelle Cobb (Wilson) was also a teacher, and she and Bo boarded together and became good friends. Nelle met and married Don W. Wilson, Jr. from there. They had three children, the oldest was their daughter, Sandra Wilson, who married Larry Chadwick from Crabapple. Nelle was Principal of Warsaw Elementary until retirement. According to Sandra, Nelle was so independent that before she became successful while living across the river from the school, she would ride a bicycle to school on pretty days. In bad weather, she would walk a half mile to catch a bus in Norcross and then meet a lady who also worked at the school and would ride the rest of the way with her, then repeat the process coming home. Nelle died in 2000, and Don in 1999.

Article in Atlanta Constitution, Sept. 4, 1938, showing Bo, as a Leader in "Youth Revivals"

> March 31, 1938.
>
> Rev. H. C. Whitener,
> Buford, Ga.
>
> My Dear Brother Whitener:
>
>   Just a word to Congratulate Mrs. Whitener on having given to the World such noble Girl. Miss Bo was with our church Sunday to put on one of the best Programs ever given by a group of young people. She even had the dignity, manners, and Spirit of her Father. I congratulate you old Man. After service we had them in our home and it was such a joy and lots of fun to have them. Having no children of our own, we rejoice to have young person come.
>
>   I am investing all I have in money, talent, time, prayers and love, in the young life of our State. I have helped nine different Boys and Girls through this year in College. Grandest work ever.
>
>   Wait, you and Mr. Fuller catch them all & send me Six Mountain Trout. Am sitting off with envy. Look for you both. I'll pray for you.
>
>   Love. Walter B. Adams.

Letter from Rev. Walter Adams written to Bo' Father,
H. C. Whitener about his Daughter, Bo

Picture of Bo's First Teaching Assignment at Duluth High School, 1938,
8th Grade; Bo is next to the end on bottom row

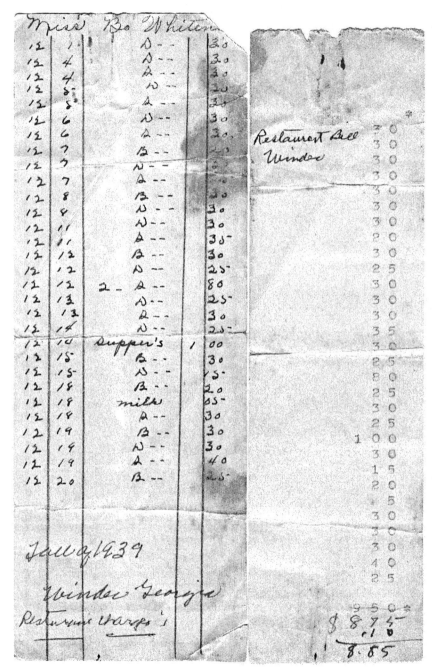

Bo's Restaurant Bill for one month while in Winder, Georgia

Louis Arden(1914-1993) & Nelle Hayes(1916-   )
—Lifelong Friends

JAMES WALTER WISE

1916 - 1938

President Georgia Baptist Student Union; Phi Beta Kappa; Phi Kappa Phi; O.D.K.; President Sigma Chi and South Eastern Balfour; Award Winner Yale and Oxford; Debater; Sophomore declamation winner; X Club Biftad: Blue Key: President Y.M.C.A.; Christian Gentleman.

Bo's Beaus

Bo's first boyfriend was Ed Anderson from her first grade class at Hickory, North Carolina. Ed sent Bo a lovely pink powder puff one year for Christmas (after they had moved again) and she always wondered what happened to the powder! He wrote in her autograph book, "I'll be loving you always, even when you are down in Georgia." From the start, she had a winning way with people, and especially with the males, with her pretty smile, curly blonde hair and friendly personality.

There were others after that, but the one Bo next remembered was her neighbor and boyfriend, Edmond Hayes, who wrote in her autograph book in 1929:

> Dearest Bo,
>   Bo when we leave dear old B.H.S. I hope you will always remember me. Bo, I wish you happiness in life. Always remember, wherever you go, I'll always love you.
>
> Love,
Ed
(The Buford "Ed")

Another time, Ed wrote: "You sure can say the sweetest things and not to mean a darn word of it—you know how alright."

And another: "I love Bo. I think that she is the sweetest girl I've ever known. Ed"
And another: "I think you are the sweetest little creature I've ever known. I think you are an angel, beautiful, wonderful and Now that's nice isn't it? Ed"

When she and Ed were in their senior year, Ed along with another classmate, William Hutchins, were riding in the back of a truck when it was struck in the rear by another vehicle, and to everyone's horror, Ed and William were instantly killed. William's father was the Whitener's doctor, and Dr. Hutchins and Rev. Whitener, made house calls together, minister for the soul and doctor for the body. The night of the accident, the doctor and the minister needed to be ministered to themselves. Edmond had given Bo a ring for Christmas, which her parents had allowed her to wear on her right hand. Bo and Edmond's "young love" ended abruptly and tragically.

On August 14, 1930, Bo saved a napkin from Sue Veach's party with Frank Adams' name written thereon.

Another interesting and amusing entry in her autograph book was by a boy named Glenn, who wrote:

> Dearest Bo:
> *You told me what to write*, but I could say it anyway. I love you with my whole soul. But I'll bet you forget those good times we had in Buford and Chattanooga in a little while. But you'd better not forget me.
>
> Always Love,
> Glenn

On March 19, 1934, Bo received this note:

> Dear Bo:
> Thanks for your immediate response to my card. Why don't you spare me this mental agony, and write me? First say that you like me. That would help.
>
> Very doubtfully your's,
> Tom

And then there were telegrams from "John," several of them, wishing "I were your colleague" and "Best of Luck on her basketball team." Another one he wrote her had this comment, "We are so different. You are miserable when you are in my presence and I am in an awful shape without you. Maybe I love you too much." Yes, John, this is called "smothering love."

There were pictures with Gradon Smith, Gordon Mein, W.R. Cannon and others.

The next young man to come into Bo's life her junior and senior years in college, was her boyfriend, Walter Wise, a wonderful young man, from Fayetteville,

Georgia. James Walter Wise of Fayetteville, was born in Washington, D.C., May 3, 1916, the son of James Walter Wise and Cora (Betts) Wise. His father represented Fayette County for several terms in the General Assembly of Georgia and served as Mayor of Fayetteville, as Solicitor-General of the Flint Judicial Circuit, and as Representative in Congress from the Sixth District of Georgia for five terms. He died in 1925.

Walter, the son, and Bo's beau, was a graduate of Fayette County High School and graduated from the University of Georgia, completing the four-year course in three years. He was cited among the top three percent in scholastic standing in the entire university system. As an outstanding student, Walter made the Sphinx (highest honors), International Debate Team, Phi Beta Kappa Honor Society, Phi Kappa Phi Fraternity, and was President of the State Baptist Student Union, and the southeast President of Sigma Chi Fraternity. Walter gave Bo his fraternity pin to wear, signifying they were sweethearts. (See photo of Walter Wise) According to Bo's written story of this that I found among her papers, they became engaged.

When Bo graduated from the University of Georgia in 1937, she was unable to attend the ceremony due to having an appendectomy and an ovary removed. When she recovered, her father, Rev. Whitener, rented a cabin at Lake Burton in the summer, and her parents allowed Bo to invite Walter Wise to go with them for a week's vacation. He was then in Law School at the UGA having graduated a year earlier. On Saturday of that week at Lake Burton, Bo's dad had to return to Buford due to being in the middle of building a new sanctuary, and the many responsibilities associated therewith.

Bo, Walt and her mother (another very unusual thing in today's world) rented a boat and motored out on the lake, with Walt as navigator. Suddenly, in the midst of a beautiful day on the lake, Walt fell back on the motor. They thought he had passed out from the sun. Bo stood and screamed until someone came to help them. Walter died in the middle of Lake Burton with a heart attack at age 21! In Bo's own words, "My world toppled!"

This was such a devastating event for all concerned, especially Bo and Walt's family when they heard the sad news. "What we once enjoyed and loved, we can never lose, for all that we love deeply becomes a part of us," Helen Keller once wrote. Sorrow can have a very purifying effect on all who are disciplined thereby. Sorrow is the great sanctifier. Sorrow can either make us better or bitter. In Bo's case, thankfully, it made her a better person.

Walt was the second boyfriend who had an untimely death. She surely asked, "Why? Walter was so young and so gifted." Again, the "why's" are in heaven with God. We won't get the answer to them until we get there.

Walt's funeral was held at First Baptist Church of Athens. The President of the University, Dr. Adams, eulogized Walter by saying that he was the most outstanding student to attend the University of Georgia. Bo sent his fraternity pin to his mother, but she returned it, saying he would want her to have it, and she still has it tucked away in her jewelry box to remind her that a wonderful guy had died, and she would always remember him. By all the activities in which he was involved, Bo knew that he was a true Christian and went to be with Jesus that day on the lake. Bo's life was about to take a different turn due to this sudden change of events. Change is another certain fact on the road of life and can be good or bad, depending upon how one approaches and accepts change. With acceptance lies peace.

Bo's father, Rev. Whitener wrote this to her upon Walt's death:

They Never Quite Leave Us by

Margaret E. Sangster

> They never quite leave us, our friends who have passed
> Through the shadows of death to the sunlight above.
> A thousand sweet memories are holding them fast
> To the places they blessed with their presence and love.
> The work which they left and the books which they read
> Speak mutely, though still with an eloquence rare,
> And the songs that they sang, the words that they said,
> Yet linger and sigh on the desolate air.
> And oft when alone, and oft in the throng,
> Or when evil allures us, or sin draweth nigh,
> A whisper comes gently, "Nay, do not the wrong,"
> And we feel that our weakness is pitied on high.

A year and a half later, Bo started dating Luke Buice. She and Luke went to the Baptist Student Union Convention at Ridgecrest in the summer. He said that he had prayed for Bo when he heard what had happened. She didn't understand all of it at the time, but in her words, "For many years it has been very clear that God was guiding and designing my life."

At Ridgecrest, she was a "house mother" to some of the students. Luke and the other men and boys stayed in a cottage about a block from the women's cottage. Bo, at that time, had been interviewed about becoming a secretary in a Baptist College for the state of Alabama, and was having a conference the next morning concerning this opportunity. All night Bo prayed, and when she got up the next morning, she knew what she was supposed to do: she was going to marry Luke Buice!! Our choices do indeed determine our destiny—not fate. Prayer was the key which unlocked the door to her new destiny. (Of course, it did help that she was at the right place at the right time to marry the right man!)

"If we will pray and not worry, we will see things change in a hurry."

—Dave Meyer

Ervin Luther Buice, I

Lela Mae Whitener (Bo)

Dies Suddenly

Shown above is Walter Wise, Fayetteville, prominent student at the University for the past four terms, who died suddenly as a result of a heart attack at Lakemont, Ga. yesterday. He was well known in Athens, having taken a leading part in young people's activities at First Baptist church.

NOTED STUDENT AT GEORGIA DIES

Walter Wise, Outstanding Religious Worker Here Passes

Walter Wise, 22, Fayetteville, one of the University of Georgia's...

Georgia Student Night Leaders

Speakers and leaders in a recent Student Night held at the First Baptist Church of Athens, Georgia, at the preaching hour. Those appearing in the picture are: Alex Saye, director of the First Church Training Union; D. B. Nicholson, of Athens, state student secretary; Miss "Bo" Whitener; Walter Wise, past president of the Georgia Student Union; and Dyer Massey, one of the student speakers. Edwin S. Preston, of Atlanta, state secretary of the Baptist Training Union Department of the Georgia Baptist Convention, also participated in the program.

—*University of Georgia, Athens.*

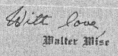
Walter Wise

WALTER WISE
FAYETTEVILLE, GA.
CANDIDATE FOR A.B. DEGREE
Sigma Chi

Phi Beta Kappa; Phi Kappa Phi; Omicron Delta Kappa; President, Sigma Chi; President, Demosthenian Literary Society; President, Baptist Student Union of Georgia; Yale Debate Trip, '34; Oxford Debate, '35; Winner Sophomore Declamation; Winner Joe Brown Connally Scholarship; "N" Club; International Relations Club; Demosthenian Key Council; Y. M. C. A. Cabinet; Biftad Club; Winner Sigma Chi Balfour Award, Southeastern Province.

The two families of Robert Graham (Bob) Buice: bottom L-R : Paul, Carl, Buddie (died at 15), Earlie

2nd row—Emory, Noah, Papa, Mama (Minnie), Luke (baby)
3rd row—Steven Ezra, Benjamin, Abraham, Marvin, Lee Luckie, George
4th row—Lillie Belle, Sidney (Sid)

This picture was probably taken late 1913 to mid 1914. Robert Graham (Bob) Buice died Feb. 15, 1915 when Luke was 21 months old.

Robert's first wife, Georgia Ann Lee Buice, married him on December 29, 1881, and they had 9 children, 8 boys and one girl. Georgia Ann died with tuberculosis on March 15, 1896 at age 34! These are their children:

Noah (1882-1953)
Emory (1883-1946)
Steven Ezra (1884-1965)
Benjamin (1886-?)
Abraham (1888-1951)

Lillie Belle (1890-1958)
Howard S. (1892-1945)
Infant (6-5-1894-8-10-94)
Infant (8-20-1895-10-5-1895)

In only three months, Robert married for the second time, Minnie Ophelia Lee, his first wife's cousin, on June 21, 1896. They also had 9 children, 8 sons and one daughter:

George (1897-1948)
Luckie (daugher) (1898-1986)
Lee (1899-1988)
Marvin (1901-1937)
Paul (1903-1986)

Carl (1905-1989)
Buddie (1907-1922)
Earlie (1910-1965)
Ervin Luther Buice (Luke)
5/16/13-8/11/01

Luke Buice

Bo met Luke Buice before Walter Wise's, Bo's former boyfriend's, death. They first met at a Sunday School Party/Picnic in Forsyth County. Luke lived down the road from his cousin, the sister of her Sunday School teacher. When Luke and his brother drove by and saw all the people having fun, they stopped "country-like" to see what was "happenin'." His cousin introduced Bo and Luke, and they went over, sat down on the roots of a big tree in the front yard, and talked and talked and talked to get acquainted. Years later they went back to visit that big tree where they first met and made a picture. Young man meets young woman, and if only that tree could talk, but we can imagine how love's arrow was hurled that day. Bo admitted that Luke was very reserved and quiet, but such a joy to be around, and even though they were opposites in temperament, they were immediately attracted to one another. She liked him that first day, but every date she had with him, she liked him even better.

That fall of 1937, after Walter Wise's death and her graduation, while Bo was teaching at Duluth High School, Luke called her and made a date to come there, saying that he had heard about Walter's death in the barber shop in Buford, and that he told himself, "maybe I will have a chance with Bo now." God's timing and will are so mysterious sometimes that we are amazed at how things happen—how one door closes and a window opens. The Good Shepherd leads His children, showing them the way, calling them by name, and counting the very hairs of their heads, the scripture declares. He leads them in and out to pasture. "My sheep hear My voice, and they follow Me," Jesus declared. So perhaps the voice Luke Buice heard wasn't his own, but actually the voice of God, leading him to "little Bo Beep" who had lost her other boyfriend to an untimely death.

To be reconciled to God's will is the challenge for us all—for His will is perfect, and nothing happens to us that is not "filtered" through His fingers of love. There is a purpose for all that we experience. God works to conform His children into His likeness—His compassion, patience, and gentle strength.

Bo remembers the first time Luke kissed her. She was living in a boarding house in Duluth when Luke came for a visit. Bo was standing on the front porch and Luke surprised her by putting his arms around her and kissing her tenderly, which she has never forgotten. Love's first kiss . . . . ah . . . . ah . . . . ah.

Tall, dark and handsome, Luke was the youngest of eight children, really sixteen, because Luke's father, Robert Graham Buice, was married twice, and Luke was the youngest of 16!! Luke's father's first wife, Georgia Ann Lee Buice, died, after having 8 children and he remarried Luke's mother, Minnie Lee, his first wife's cousin, and they had 8 more children. There was one girl in each set. Luke's sister was named "Luckie."

Luke's father, Robert (Bob) Graham Buice, died on February 15, 1915 at the age of 53, when Luke was just 21 months old. His mother, Minnie, was one of those rugged women of yore who, with great faith in God, managed to raise her large family, and was quite successful, despite all the hardships and lack of money. She inherited a small farm, and bought a small grocery store, where she and the older children worked. This, in turn, made it possible for the younger children to go to school and then to college.

I talked with Frances Hudson, Earlie Buice's daughter, who now lives in Washington, Georgia. She and I marveled together at all the facts of this intriguing family. She told me of a story her dad had told her of her Grandmother Minnie cutting pencils in half for all the children, and giving the older children the "half-pencils" with the erasers, and the younger children the other halves. She also said that when the children went to school in the Sharon Community of Forsyth County on what is now Old Atlanta Road, she packed all their lunches in one large washtub! They raised most of their own food. To look back, they were underprivileged in so many ways, but they were also blessed and privileged to have had a godly mother who kept on keeping on, despite hardship and struggle. Can you imagine the work involved in raising that many children alone, after her husband had died? She had to have had divine help to have survived. Actually, she did a fantastic job. Frances said that she never heard her grandmother complain about anything. Minnie never cooked on Sundays, according to Frances, but cooked enough on Saturdays to prepare for Sundays. She took literally the scriptural mandate to remember the Sabbath by keeping it holy. And let's face it, this lady needed a rest when Sunday rolled around!

Luke's mom inherited a farm in Forsyth County to rear those eight+ children, and Bo has marveled through the years to hear how they all lived and worked together to grow their own food and to get an education. To look back, in so many ways, they were underprivileged, but in other ways, they were privileged and refined. Luke's godly mother didn't have any formal education, but she managed to get a little store, which Luke eventually followed in her footsteps, and the older boys worked in the little store, making it possible for the younger boys to go to college, following high school at Cumming, Georgia. Luke graduated with honors from Cumming High School in 1932. Lee Buice, Luke's older brother who became his "father image" and some of the older boys became acquainted with the President of Piedmont College in Demorest, Georgia who allowed the younger boys to come to school on a scholarship. This was a miracle in those days as much as it would be today. But God had his hand on Luke Buice from the very beginning.

Luke was elected President of the student body at Piedmont in 1936 and played basketball in 1935-36. He graduated from Piedmont College Cum Laude in 1936 with a B.A. degree. He was listed among the Who's Who Among Students in American Colleges and Universities of 1935-36; as "Honorary Scholarship based on Scholastic Attainments and Character;" Sec. and Pres. of the Protropian Society; Advertising Man of Year Book; Vice Pres. of the U.M.C.A.; Pres. of Student's Assoc. Hobbies: Music, Singing, Outdoor sports.

Next Luke taught and coached at Commerce High School in 1936-37. He later received his Master's Degree from the University of Georgia in 1942 with a M.A. in Academics.

From the Buice children, there were three preachers: Lee, Marvin and George. Four were Principals of schools: Carl, Luke, George and Lee. Three were school teachers at one time: Marvin, Earlie and Luke. His older brother, Lee Buice, like a father to Luke, was Pastor of Roswell First Baptist before Bo and Luke were married. He served Crestview Church in Marietta, and Lincolnton and Goshen churches. Lee Buice was a graduate of Piedmont College, Mercer University and Southern Seminary. He was a public school teacher and Principal of Duluth High School before becoming a minister. He married Adelia Staton of Lincolnton, and had one daughter, Adelia Buice Snellings, who also had two daughters, all of Lincolnton.

Luke's brother, Carl, became the Principal at Sugar Hill, near Buford, Georgia and a building was named for him, which building eventually burned. George, another brother, also became a minister of the gospel in a little country church outside of Roswell. Several of the boys sang in a quartet, "The Buice Brother's Quartet" and made several albums under the Columbia label. Marvin, Paul, Carl and Luke or Earlie all participated at one time or another in this wonderful ministry. (See photo) The Buice Brother's Quartet sang all over the state of Georgia for then Senator Richard B. Russell.

Luke, age 26, was teaching English at Winder High School, when he asked Bo, age 24, to marry him, and Bo readily accepted and they were wed at Christmastime, December 24, 1939 at the Buford First Baptist Church, the first couple to be married in the new sanctuary there. Ironically, Alan and I were the first couple to be married in the new sanctuary at Roswell First Baptist Church in 1964, twenty five years later, at which time, I came to meet Luke and Bo, and to be in the Sunday School Class that she taught for young women.

Bo wore a three-quarter length, waltz blue dress to her wedding. She said laughing, "Crazy me, I kept it and still have it after all these years—but after three years, it had 'yellowed,' so I dyed it black! O mercy. Yes sir, I remember going to J.P. Allen's and looking for that dress just like it was yesterday. Law, law. My father married Luke and me, and Horace, my brother, who was eight years younger, nudged and teased me while we were walking down the isle together."

Bo's maid of honor was her sister, Clarice, and Luke's preacher brother, Lee, was the best man, plus Bo's childhood friend, Nelle Hayes, Cary Wheeler, a BSU friend, and her cousin, Tommie Hopkins, were the other attendants. Luke Green, one of the groomsman, was later editor of one of Atanta's newspapers, At this point Bo got nostalgic realizing that most of these people are dead now, all except for her and Nelle Hayes. What would it be like to outlive so many of your family and friends? She felt the pain as she was remembering and smiled that beautiful smile of her's.

Luke and Bo honeymooned that night at the Winecoff Hotel at 176 Peachtree Street in Atlanta, which hotel later burned in 1946, when 119 people were killed. The Hotel had been built in 1913, the year Clarice was born. Bo and Luke left on Christmas Day, 1939, for their honeymoon in New Orleans. As they rode happily down the road, Bo turned around to look in the back seat, noticing no luggage!! In their haste and excitement to leave, they had forgotten their luggage, and had to retrace the 40 miles they'd traveled. They enjoyed spending a great week together, however, when they finally arrived to their destination. She still remembers how the downtown area of New Orleans surprised her, this little "protected" girl from Georgia.

They came back to Buford and said goodbye to her parents, and then moved to Winder where they both taught school. There they rented an apartment in the home of a sweet lady. After several nights there, Bo was terrified by what she had never seen before: bedbugs!! They then moved to Ms. Almond's, across the street from Judge Pratt. They boarded until Luke was elected to teach English at Swainsboro High, and Bo taught there one year, also.

Oh, the adventures of young lovers. They are dazzled by life and what it has to offer them. This is one reason God wants us to remain "young at heart," but not "childish." To be "young at heart" is to remain open to new ideas and new adventures, to remain childlike in our outlook and be teachable. To stay "childish" and not mature keeps us bound to the past and not able to move on with God. Luke and Bo continued to face the future with confidence and belief that God was directing their steps—and their stops!!

Our Pastor Ron Bradley's daughter, Amber, told Bo, "I hope when I'm your age, I'll be just like you!" She was referring to Bo's "young heart" which she has kept through the years.

Luke's Family
back: Marvin, Lee, Carl & Paul Buice;
front: Earlie, Minnie, Luke & Aunt Katie

bottom picture:
The Buice Brothers' Singers, 1938:
Lee, Carl, Earlie, Paul & Luke

The Old Buice Store, which burned in 2005,
in Forsyth Co., Georgia
(We think this was Minnie's Store back in the early 1900's)

Luke & Bo's First year of Marriage, 1940

Whitener-Buice Troth Is Told

Announcement is made today by the Rev. and Mrs. H. C. Whitener, of Buford, of the engagement of their daughter, Bo Whitener, to Erwin Luther Buice, of Winder, the marriage to be solemnized in December.

The bride-elect is a graduate of Buford High School and of the University of Georgia, where she was a member of Alpha Gamma Delta, social sorority, and Kappa Delta Pi, honorary scholastic fraternity. She also was a member of the cabinet of the Voluntary Religious Association. She is now a member of the faculty of the Winder Junior High School. Her mother was before her marriage Miss Lela White, of Chattanooga. On the maternal side she is the granddaughter of the late Mr. and Mrs. John Sterman White, of Cleveland, Tenn. On her paternal side she is the granddaughter of the late W. T. Whitener, of Chattanooga, and the late Mr. Whitener.

Mr. Buice is the son of Mrs. R. G. Buice, of Suwanee, and the late Mr. Buice. He was graduated from Piedmont College, where he served as president of the student body. While in school he was a member of the glee club and of the Y. M. C. A. cabinet. He is at present a member of the faculty of the Winder High School.

MISS BO WHITENER

MISS BO WHITENER WILL W[ED] MR. BUICE AT DECEMBER RITES

Widespread interest throughout the state is centered in the announcement made by the Rev. and Mrs. H. C. Whitener of Buford, of the engagement of their daughter, Miss Bo Whitener, to Erwin Luther Buice, of Winder. The marriage will be solemnized in December.

The bride-elect is a graduate of the Buford High school and of the University of Georgia, where she was a member of Alpha Gamma Delta social sorority and Kappa Phi honorary scholastic fraternity. She also was a member of the cabinet of the Voluntary Religious Association, and was outstanding in Baptist student work. She is now a member of the faculty of the Winder Junior High school.

Her mother was before her marriage, Miss Lela White, of Chattanooga, Tenn. On her maternal side she is the granddaughter of the late Mr. and Mrs. John Sterman White of Cleveland, Tenn.

On her paternal side she is the granddaughter of Mrs. W. E. Whitener of Chattanooga, Tenn, and the late Mr. Whitener.

Mr. Buice is the son of Mrs. R. G. Buice, of Suwanee and the late Mr. Buice. He was graduated from Piedmont College where he served as president of the student body. While in school he was a member of the Glee Club and of the Y. M. C. A. cabinet. He is at present a member of the faculty of the Winder High school.

Luke & Bo under the Old Oak Tree, 1953

Ervin Luther (Luke) Buice in WWII

Luke, Bo & Baby Ervin, 1944

Ervin Luther Buice, I And II

IF YOU HAVE A LITTLE BOY—

If you have a little boy
    All your very own,
Then you have enough and more
    To make a happy home.

And if but once a day
    You should see him smile,
That would be enough and more
    To make your life worthwhile.

Or, say you have a little boy
    To read to every night,
That would be enough and more
    To make your evenings bright.

And if each night at bed time
    You can kiss this little lad,
That will be enough and more
    To make you very glad.

And if you see him in the evening
    When he kneels to pray,
That will be enough and more
    To make a perfect day.

    —Oma Carlyle Anderson
    from The American Album of Poetry
    by Ted Malone

The year Luke and Bo married, 1939, Luke was teaching in Winder and Bo at Duluth High School. Bo was then chosen to teach at Winder also. The next year she taught at a rural school because the schools in the Winder city limits did not allow married women to teach! Hard to believe how things have changed—some for the better, some worse.

Bo next taught sixth and seventh grades in Sandersville, Georgia in 1941 and 42 while Luke taught English in High School there and was elected Principal of the school in early 1942. Each time they moved, Luke got a promotion. Next, the young couple moved to Walterboro, South Carolina. While there, Uncle Sam drafted Luke into World War II. Bo went back to live with her parents. This was the year 1942. Luke trained and lived at Harvard School of Communication for about six months in Cambridge, Massachusetts for officer's training. Luke rented an apartment for Bo. They both enjoyed touring that historic part of the United States on his "off" time. He was commissioned an Ensign in the U.S. Navy that same year.

From Massachusetts, Luke was sent to San Diego, California, in preparation for his being shipped to the South Pacific. Bo joined him in California and became secretary at the Arden Dairy Farm, where people were so kind and caring of them.

Bo's parents told Luke before they married that the doctors had told them that Bo couldn't have children, but as Bo wrote, "Nobody told me!" So one day four years after they had been married, Luke and Bo were walking and talking in Balboa Park in San Diego, and Bo said to him, "Honey, I'm 29 years old, and if I'm going to have baby, I want to have one now." When Bo decided she wanted a baby and prayed about it, God answered affirmatively. When she became pregnant, the doctor first thought she had a tumor since she only had one ovary. The miracle baby, Ervin Luther Buice II, was born on June 17th, 1944. Luke presented Bo with a beautiful opal ring at Ervin's birth, which ring she wears faithfully everyday since that day. In Bo's words, "Have you met that 'impossible' baby? I could never tell you what joy he has given to us." (I was born the same day in Atlanta.)

Luke was attached to the Naval Sound School in San Diego and was sent from there to the South Pacific as Communications' Officer aboard the ship, U.S.S. Rocky Mount. Bo will never forget the day, holding her baby of one month, and seeing that ship depart with her loving Luke aboard, leaving her to face the future and the world alone. But God had not left her, because He promises never to leave us nor forsake us. Bo has hundreds of Luke's letters during their time of separation. He wrote her almost every day!

Cleve Whitener, Bo's dad, came out on the train to get Bo and little Erv and drove them back to Georgia in her T-model Ford, stopping at service stations and restaurants to warm Erv's formula. Ervin even gained a pound on their trip from San Diego, California, to Buford, Georgia. When Erv was perhaps 11 months' old, Bo met Luke at the airport, and remembers Luke seeing his baby for only the second time and reaching out, and Ervin, of course, didn't know his Dad, and Erv kind of drew back. Luke got to stay on furlough for a short time before having to return. Bo and Ervin stayed in Brookhaven with her parents, Mr. and Mrs. Whitener.

God also protected Luke through three major invasions in which his ship was involved during the war. The Rocky Mount, named for the Rocky Mountains, was commissioned on October 15, 1943, and sailed for Pearl Harbor, via the Panama Canal, arriving on December 27 and stayed there until January 10, 1944. The Rocky Mount reached Saipan on June 15, the day the attack on Mariannas Islands was scheduled to begin and (two days prior to Ervin's birth, by the way). Enemy air attack was constant and heavy throughout the operation, and while ships all around were either hit or under direct attack, the Rocky Mount came through untouched. Organized resistance on Saipan ceased after 24 days.

In July, 1944 when Ervin was six weeks old, Luke boarded the Rocky Mount with Task Unit 52.18.18, and got underway and proceeded toward Guam for the assault and capture of that island. The beaches were secured quickly, and four days later the ship departed from Guam for the assault and capture of Tinian Island. The ship then returned to Saipan, and on August 15, she set sail again for Pearl Harbor, arriving there on August 26. On September 15, the ship sailed for Manus and on October 14, left Manus for the assault and capture of Leyte in the Philippine Islands, where she participated in shore bombardment. Enemy air attack was continuous throughout this operation, but God's hand of protection was on them.

The Rocky Mount with Luke aboard, then sailed to Hollandia, Dutch New Guinea, observing landing operations, undergoing gunnery practices and drills. On January 6, 1945, the ship returned to the Philippines to participate in the Lingayen operation, and was under frequent air attack and constant aerial observation. After almost five weeks there, she departed for Leyte in company with two Australian men-of-war and two U.S. Destroyers. Following a brief rest in Leyte, on March 5 and got underway again on March 8 for landings on Zamboanga, Mindanao, P.I.

Mortar fire, directed at the beached ships became very heavy. Shortly after noon, Major General Doe and his staff left the ship to set up headquarters and take command on shore. Two weeks after the operation began, the Rocky Mount left the assault area and departed again for Subic Bay. On April 4, the ship got underway again for Morotai Island, where all hands attended memorial services for the late President, Franklin D. Roosevelt.

The next assignment for the ship was Tarakan Island, Borneo and they got underway on April 23, 1945. During shore bombardment, a large ammunition dump blew up, with an explosion so intense that ships in the transport area were shaken by the blast—but the Rocky Mount and all those aboard were protected again!

On May 3, she weighed anchor to return to Morotai Island for a brief relaxation period. Luke got a furlough sometime near here and met Bo and Ervin, who was then 11 months old. (See photo) Other routine operations continued until 2100 on August 10, 1945 when the Domei News reported that the Japanese Government had accepted the Potsdam Terms, with fireworks and celebration until midnight.

The ship proceeded to Manila, then on to Jinsen, Korea on September 10. The next day, she left for the Yellow Sea and on to the Yangtze River, where she anchored on September 15 until minesweepers had swept the channel to Shanghai clean. However, to avoid a typhoon, the ship hurriedly put to sea and returned after three days of riding rough seas and anchored off the mouth of the Yangtze.

On September 19, the Rocky Mount led the U.S. and Allied Ships, the first Allied ship in four years to make the passage up the Yangtze and Whangpoo Rivers. The shores were lined with crowds who cheered, waved flags and exploded fire crackers. Whistles blew and the noise was deafening as the Rocky Mount led the fleet back to Shanghai.

Thus ended the World War II fighting career of the U.S.S. Rocky Mount, third of the Auxiliary, General Communications class ships. From the time she arrived at Pearl Harbor on the 27 of December, 1943 she never left the combat area of the Pacific. Although exposed to bombs, torpedoes, and shells, she came through all of her operations unscathed. Her record of continuous combatant service and nine amphibious operations justifies the claim of "The Rock" as the "Veteran Queen of the Amphibious Fleets." For her service during World War II, Rocky Mount earned six battle stars, and the Navy Unit Commendation. Luke survived along with his ship and returned to San Diego for his Naval discharge at Thanksgiving, 1945 when Ervin was 1 ½ years old.

(I would like to credit Tim Combs, now deceased, for obtaining all this information.) (see Photo)

While Luke was in the Pacific, Bo and Ervin returned to Georgia to live with her parents in Brookhaven. After having served the Buford Baptist Church for almost 20 years, Rev. Whitener was elected Secretary of Evangelism for the Georgia Baptist Convention, and he and Mrs. Whitener moved to Brookhaven. Mercer University conferred the Doctorate Degree to Rev. Whitener soon afterwards.

Bo didn't teach during this time, due to caring for their adorable baby boy, who was a year and a half when Luke returned. Luke got a job with the Veteran's Administration in 1946 and 1947, but he and his brother, Earlie, bought a business together that year in Roswell, the Economy Auto Store, later named Otasco. In 1952, Luke bought the business, and it was owned by him for the next 27 years before the mega-giants, Walmart and Home Depot, became popular. He first opened his store next to Ollie Mae Thomas' Beauty Shop on Elizabeth Way in Roswell. Next, he moved to the building where Reeves Grocery Store used to be on the hill on Canton Street where the Antique Mall is today. The third move was where the fire department used to be and finally, he moved to the present location of Ace Hardware on Atlanta Street. Luke and Hershel David bought the Atlanta Street property together, but Luke eventually bought it from Hershel. Luke sold Otasco and retired in 1979. Bo retired one year later.

When they first moved to Roswell in 1947, Luke and Bo rented a house on Canton Street across from Hobo's Service Station, next door to Dorcas and Rucker McDonald's grandmother's home. It was in front of Mr. Farr's, Joy Farr Lackey's grandfather. "Such fine people," Bo commented. She and Luke stayed there for a short time until their present home at 83 Bulloch Avenue was built in 1950 when Ervin was 6 years old. Mr. Jessie Butler's sister, Sybil Butler, owned the property and sold it to them. Art Cowart was their builder, and did an excellent job. They added a family room in the 70's. Some water pipes had to be replaced in the basement this year (2005), but it is still a wonderful house to this day.

Concerning her marriage to Luke Buice, Bo said, "There was never a better man on earth other than Jesus, than Luke Buice. He was so good to me and others. Marrying Luke was one of the best decisions I ever made." She went on to tell how at Christmastime, when people couldn't pay for their toys on lay-away at his store, he delivered them anyway. Bo has a letter in her possession in which someone wrote to him about stealing something from his store. Years later, when this individual was saved from his/her sins, and found the Lord Jesus, this person wrote to Luke that the "The Holy Spirit" had brought conviction and remembrance of the theft, apologized and made restitution by returning the $10 which the item cost. The letter ended, "I have wished many times that I had not done it, but I did. I am not going to sign this letter, and I want you to know that I never used the item I stole. It was either lost, or stolen from me, but I never saw it again after putting it in my car after taking it from you in your store." Luke Buice was the kind of businessman who generated this type of response from his customers. His goodness endured through the years to all who knew him and had contact with him. He was honest and kind, hard working and caring. He didn't have to lie, cheat nor steal to become successful. Oh, how young men need to follow his example of success: show up and be good to others, work hard and be faithful. Luke kept his priorities straight: God, family, and work in that order.

Luke Buice started the first scholarship fund at Piedmont College, and as did his close friend, Dr. Horace Sturgess, later President of Kennesaw College. Luke won a voice scholarship, and loved good literature, music, poetry and spiritual things. He was a giver and a gentle man, who demonstrated Christlikeness. The former head custodian at Roswell First Baptist, James Moore, who also shares the same birthday as Ervin and me, said that when he first saw Luke, he thought that he would be a "racist." But was he wrong! One Sunday while James was walking down the hall during the Sunday School hour, Luke saw him and invited him to join his class, which he did, and was a member for many years. James is still a good friend and helps Bo from time to time with odd jobs.

The only difference that Bo and Luke ever had was that she was more "social-minded" and he was more "retiring." She wanted to go more that he did. If they ever disagreed, he would just look at her and smile. Margaret Ovbey said that Luke would just roll his eyes. Never once in their 61-year marriage did he say an unkind remark to her. "He wouldn't have harmed anybody," she declared. Bo said they were truly "equally-yoked" in their marriage, spiritually, and were truly "one." They were both interested in the church, and spiritual matters. She advises young people of faith to be so careful to marry within the faith in order to ensure happiness.

Luke's religious and civic activities included Deacon, Roswell First Baptist Church, Sunday School Superintendent, Adult Sunday School Teacher, Soloist and Choir Member, Rotarian, Member Pro-Mozart Society of Atlanta, Board Member of the Shoe String Opera Company in Atlanta, Member Roswell Historical Society, Member Atlanta Area Piedmont Alumni Club; his hobby was gardening.

Luke was very romantic and would tell Bo, "Hon, you have the prettiest hands I've ever seen." He called her, "Baby," and was so tender and wrote her personal notes, leaving them where she would find them. His mother must have instilled in her children the love of the Heavenly Father. Luke said things to her to build her up and these would make her so happy. Especially as you get older, Bo says, how women need that tenderness. If men loved their wives as Christ has instructed them to and wives respected their husbands, we could have a revival in America's families!! (See Ephesians, Chapter Five)

You say, "But you don't know my wife (or husband). She (or he) is so "mean and hateful" or so "indifferent," so "unromantic," Yes, I know. That is because of the sin nature which we inherited from our parents, Adam and Eve. But, when we are "born again" into God's family, and ask Jesus to live in our hearts by faith, Jesus gives us a new nature. His Holy Spirit comes to live inside of us, enabling us to love the unlovable, to speak words of gentleness and kindness, to overlook the faults of others, and to be Christlike in our attitudes and relationships. Some of us are harder to train than others because of our backgrounds, but Jesus is the One who does the changing. It is very difficult for us to change ourselves and impossible to change others. We can only rest in Him, abide in Him and allow

Him to do the changing. There is hope for all our relationships to improve because of the difference He can make in our lives and marriages. The old saying goes, "Practice makes perfect," and this applies even to our relationships.

Bo saved many of the cards and letters Luke wrote her through their 61 years together. This is one that he wrote to Bo in his beautiful handwriting:

> To my Bo, the love of my life:
> For I love you, truly, truly, dear.
> May today and everyday be filled with wishes come true. Happy Birthday. I remember the prayer as we were parked in a little nook in my '35 Chevrolet at Ridgecrest in the summer of '39. My prayer was that our lives might be together as our hearts were at that time. That prayer is still being answered every day,
>
> Luke

Love letter from Luke to Bo

The Rock

USS Rocky Mount (AGC-3)

The Rocky Mt., Luke's ship in WWII

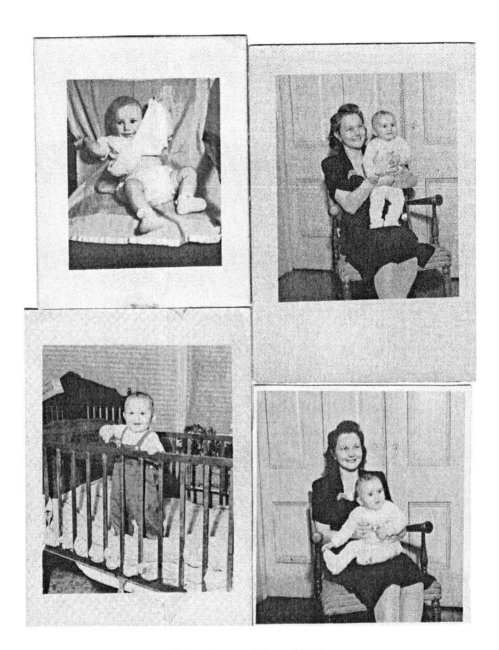

Baby pictures of Bo and Ervin

Buice Family when Luke returned home from the war

Ervin's little choir robe that his grandmother Lela made for him

NOON

Ervin Buice & Eddie Sullivan, Lifelong Friends,
2001 RHS Reunion

On Ervin and Friendship

In 1944 and 45, while Luke was in the South Pacific fighting the Japanese, and while she was living with her parents, who attended First Baptist Atlanta, Bo joined Brookhaven Baptist Church just two blocks from their home, and which was pastored by Rev. Fred Thomas. There Bo made good friends, including Bill and Elizabeth Turner and Garney Thomas, Fred's wife, with whom Bo remains close friends today, 60 years later. While teaching a Sunday School Class of Young Women at Brookhaven, she made so many good friends including Elizabeth who told Bo recently, "Bo, you have so many more friends than I do." Bo said to me, "Linda, that is so important, to be a friend so that you will have friends until the end. And try to do good. When I pray, I ask that God will still use me to be a blessing to others."

A quote on a pillow in Bo's favorite chair reads: "It takes a long time to grow an old friend." Then I read this one in a book: "Count your blessings by smiles, not tears; count your age by friends, not years." St. Thomas Aquinas is credited with saying, "There is nothing on this earth more to be prized than true friendship." So many people when they get older just drop out, but that only makes life harder. We invest in people, so that when we get older, we still have people in our lives. This is something Bo did beautifully.

Bo's relationships with so many people can be attributed to her ability to love people the way they are, to accept them unconditionally, to see the good in them always. Friendship is "a promise made in the heart, unbreakable by distance, and unchangeable by time," an unknown author has written. Bo taught her son well about people skills, because he, too, had so many friends everywhere he went and kept in touch in his friendly way. Ervin Luther Buice II, named for his father, was such a wonderful young man, full of energy, gifted, with a very winning personality, a contagious, and hardy laugh like his grandfather, Cleve.

While Bo and Ervin were living with her parents in Brookhaven, she took Ervin to the Cherub Choir at First Baptist Atlanta for vocal instruction under the excellent director of music, Mr. Ray Smathers. "O Master Let Me Walk With Thee" was just one of the many solos that young Ervin sang in these early years while standing on a little box, referred to by Mr. Smathers as "the little box," which went everywhere they sang! Ervin's grandmother, Lela, made his little robe. She also made a little white shirt for him from one of Cleve's shirts! Bo continued to take Ervin back to sing in the Cherub Choir after they moved to Roswell, and in the choir is where he first met MaryEm Robinson, who was later to play a very important role in his life. **(See photos)**

Those of us who went through school with Ervin, beginning in kindergarten, knew him as a good friend. Bo doesn't think that he had to be spanked but very few times in those growing up years. She said that he always came into the house singing, and his laughter was infectious. He made everyone laugh, because he came from a very stable home, where there was lots of love and laughter. Even as a little boy, he was "happy go lucky" and would evoke laughter from his parents, friends, relatives, teachers and others. He just liked people and people liked him. Sometimes Luke and Bo would try to get him to be quieter in his talking and laughter, but that was like telling Niagara Falls to be quiet!

Ervin attended kindergarten at the home of Mrs. Heath Rushin. Norma Fields (Hawkins) and Nan Anglin (Eubanks), whom Bo taught in the seventh grade, would go across the street from Roswell Elementary to get Ervin from kindergarten, where he attended with Merrill Rushin, Mary Lee Dolvin, and me among others. Norma would say to Bo, "He's been acting up again!"

Unfortunately, life has a way of turning our laughter into tears at certain times in our lives. We have to have both to make our lives complete. Bo had two miscarriages plus thyroid surgery when Ervin was still young. She remembers him standing over her following the surgery, and it just broke her heart to hear him say, "Mother, it doesn't show; everything will be alright." He always had a heart of compassion for others, which just flowed through his veins!

There never was a dull moment when Ervin was around. I remember one time in grammar school at Roswell Elementary, in one class that we shared, someone got sick and vomited. While all the rest of us were gagging and complaining, Ervin ran down the hall, got a mop and bucket and started cleaning up the mess. He was that kind of guy. He cared about others.

From a former classmate of mine and Ervin's, Richard Reeves, who now lives in Boulder, Colorado, I received the following e-mail on Aug. 21, 2005:

> *Linda,*
> *"Two very small, brief events always come to mind when I think of Ervin. Not one of the episodes is particularly significant but taken together they show a pattern of how quietly kind and sensitive Ervin was. Both incidents occurred at the Roswell First Baptist Church.*

One Sunday Ervin and I were sitting next to one another in the choir loft during service. Although in hindsight I am certain that it was not a sudden onset, at the time, I just broke out in a fever during the service, alternating between chills and sweat. Some might have just chalked it up to the Lord trying to grab my soul, but Ervin saw that I was sick. Because the service was nearing its end and it would have been embarrassing to walk out of the choir loft, I suffered. While many would have sympathized with my plight, Ervin did more. As I shivered, he moved closer in an effort to keep me warm, taking my hands and rubbing them vigorously trying to create a little heat. I remember thinking how kind and thoughtful this simple gesture was and, in looking back, I cannot once think of an unkind moment caused by Ervin in all the years I was in Roswell.

The second incident was during choir practice. Despite my sometimes boisterous manner, I was an extremely shy person. Our new choir director asked each of us to sing a song—alone—so that he might learn our capabilities. I was not expecting such a challenge and could never have sung by myself. After a moment of awkward silence when the director called on me, Ervin stood up and said,'Let me sing with Richard.' So, we sang a duet and I was saved the humiliation of being banned from the choir.

There are countless memories of Ervin, but these two have always meant the most to me personally."

Richard

From Melanie Iseman Still, who wanted to say that he wasn't perfect, and also had some mischievousness :

"I remember in the seventh grade, if you had an outside patrol post, you got to go in the clinic when you got back to school, to dry off or warm up. It was there that Ervin learned how to stick his hand in the Coke machine and pull out a Coke. But one day the mechanism rolled around and caught his wrist! He was already tall at this age, and he was standing there bent over, saying, 'If you guys go off and leave me, I'm gonna get ya!!'"

I always told my sons, "You'll always get caught when doing something wrong because you have a praying mom." So did Ervin.

When Ervin and Eddie Sullivan were put together in the same classroom, the teacher had a real challenge on her hands. The two of them together were like Bud Abbott and Lou Costello. They were hilarious!! They kept us all in stitches with their antics and their impersonations. Ervin was born to entertain folks. Mrs. Buice remembers the fun Ervin and Eddie had at their house after school, playing basketball, laughing and "hanging out" together. Writers write, teachers teach, artists paint and entertainers entertain!! Ervin "entertained" his fellow classmates from his earliest years. He was very popular and outgoing to say the least. Ervin referred to Eddie as the brother he never had, and he wrote a poem to Eddie on his 50th birthday: "50 on the Front . . . . Now, It's On to the Back-Nine." **(See poem at end of chapter)**

Ervin was also very athletic—played both football and basketball in high school and went to state competitions in track and field. The coaches loved him because he was very adept in athletics and academics. I can still see him walking down the halls of Roswell High School with Mr. Charles Newton or Mr. Bob Campbell, laughing and sharing their love for sports and World History.

Ervin was voted President of the Junior Class at Roswell High School and he and I were voted "Most Versatile" Senior Superlatives, Class of 1962, and were both Honor Graduates. We were always good friends. I loved him because he always made me laugh and was so glad to see me when we would have the opportunity. Myrt Knuckles, Bo and Luke's maid, from Roswell also worked for my mother occasionally, and she said she'd always hoped he and I would get together, but we were more like brother and sister than boyfriend and girlfriend.

My Aunt Gladys and Uncle Jake Coleman, good friends of the Buice's, first introduced Mert to them. Ervin was four years old, when Myrt started ironing for them and Myrt said, "I ironed for years and years for them, and Ervin had the sweetest little clothes, and I loved ironing them. Mrs. Buice didn't buy a lot but what she bought was good stuff. He had these two little pair of shoes, one for Sunday and one for everyday—and the cutest little overcoat and a cap to match which she kept for years and years." When Ervin got to be a "big" boy (around 6), they moved to the present address at 83 Bulloch Avenue and she often cooked dinner. One of Bo's greatest regrets is that she never took the time to teach Myrt to read. (Myrt is 85 at the writing of this book, and is a resident of Roswell Nursing Home on Green Street. She is bedridden, but her spirit is free and her mind is still sharp.) Ervin served as a pallbearer at Myrt's husband's "homegoing," and was touched to have been asked. Wearing the white gloves with the other men, it was an honor for him to try to return some of the love Myrt had given all those years. **(See Photo of Myrt at end of chapter)**

Upon graduation from Roswell High School in 1962, Ervin won four scholarships: The New England Conservatory, The Cincinnati Conservatory of Music, a voice plus track scholarship to Furman University, and The University of Georgia. He chose Furman. Mr. Dupree Rhame was the Director of Music at Furman, and early on he "discovered" Ervin's God-given musical ability. Ervin sang the first solo in the Messiah at Furman that had ever been sung by a student there. Scholastically, Ervin did not stay as interested as he had in high school, because he was traveling with the choral group all over the state singing and was "wrapped up" totally in music from that time forth. He received his Bachelor's Degree in Voice from Furman University and a Master's Degree in Voice and

Opera Performance from the New England Conservatory of Music in Boston, Massachusetts.

He began his career at Theater Under the Stars at Chastain Park following graduation. Alan and I attended and I remember how excited we were and went back stage to greet him. That same season, Ervin made his operatic debut in *La Traviata* with Dorothy Kirsten, Richard Tucker and Robert Merrill. He later shared the stage with opera greats such as Richard Tucker and Robert Merrill in New York.

Ervin sang *"Till the End of Time"* at our wedding (Alan Martin and Linda Mansell—see photo) at Roswell First Baptist Church on June 6, 1964. Rev. Brantley Seymour, my Pastor at the time, officiated. As I've said before, we were the first couple to be married in the new sanctuary.

Following graduation from Furman in 1966, in August of that year, Ervin married Judi Fredericks whom he met there. Her father was a Baptist Minister from New Jersey.

In the early 70's, when Ervin and Judi were visiting friends, Bob (his artistic director) and Sally, the discussion came up about his name. People couldn't pronounce it correctly, and that night is when Ervin made the decision to get a "theatrical" name. He chose "Jason" and changed the spelling of "Buice" to "Byce." Yes, his parents understood why, but they were hurt by this decision as any parent would be. Those of us who were his friends, also had a difficult time adjusting to the change, and would flip back and forth from "Ervin" to "Jason." He legally changed it sometime in the 80's.

Ervin served in the United States Army during the Vietnam War in the 60's. It was there that he made a great friend, Bill Ivey, from California. (See his letter at the end of the chapter). They were two of the fortunate ones who came home from Vietnam, like Ervin's father, Luke, before him who also returned safely from World War II. Unfortunately, during their time there, Ervin and Bill, among many others, were exposed to "Agent Orange." (Agent Orange is a defoliating agent used to spray villages during the Vietnam War in order to clear the area thus enabling the American Soldiers to better see the enemy. The agent was used beween 1962 and 1971 and reached it's peak in 1967-1968, while Jason was there. As a result of their contact with the AO, the poisonous agent got into the blood stream of the American Soldiers and has had a deadly affect on their IMMUNINE SYSTEMS. So, that's the reason that 30 years later they are dying! In the years following the war many Veterans have suffered from ailments which the VA attributes to the Agent Orange but, more specifically to the poisonous Dioxin in it. The following illnesses are recognized by the VA as being directly associated to their contact with Agent Orange. Chloracne, Non-Hodgkin's Lymphoma, Soft tissue sarcoma, Hodgkin's Disease, Porphyria Cutanea Tarda (PCT), Multiple Myeloma, Respiratory cancers, Prostate cancer, Peripheral neuorapthy, Type 2 Diabetes. Also, Spina bifida, and other birth defects have occurred in the children of Women Vetnam Veterans.)

Ervin and Judi came to our home and spent New Years' Eve with us one year when our sons were small. I remember Ervin teasing me about my sausage patties that I prepared for an early breakfast, calling them "brownies." His boisterous laughter and tall statue frightened our young sons, but they grew to love and respect him when they grew older. Rusty, Tony and Ryan, our sons, thought he was a "giant," which he proved to be in his own way—the gentle giant we all loved.

Sadly, Ervin and Judi's marriage ended after just nine years. Judi accepted his singing career, and they both felt like failures in their marriage breakup, but they did remain friends. They both needed time to "grow up." In an e-mail to me, Judi wrote, "He was a great guy and I have fond memories of him."

After Judi, Ervin married Jada Corbett, a flight attendant for TWA. They were married on a yacht as it cruised off the coast of Marina Del Re, California on April 12, 1984, with Bo, Luke and Cat and close friends including TV star, Shirley Jones, Elke Sommer (of *The Pink Panther* fame) in attendance. The marriage was performed by Dr. Jess Moody, Jason's Pastor at The Shepherd of the Hills Baptist Church in the San Fernando Valley. One of Jason's most cherished snapshots was one of Jess, his son, Patrick, and Jason all sitting on a bench in front of their church. Jason affectionately entitled the picture: "the Father, Son and the Holy Terror." Jada and Jason's marriage also ended after a very short time. Ironically, Jada's first husband, Harvey, and Ervin (Jason) became best friends and spent much time together.

Jason always knew what he wanted to do—perform on the stage, but he couldn't always do it. You must make money to live, so he had struggles as many performers before and after him learn rather quickly, and Bo didn't know it until later the trials that he went through to do what he loved. Ervin had a little dog, Captain, and when he was out west working in some of the plays there, he told her that one time he actually ate some of the dog food! It nearly killed Bo because she would have given him "the last shirt off her back." But he was so proud, he didn't ask, and on his behalf, parents shouldn't constantly rescue their children when the going gets rough. If they do, the children do not learn to depend upon God.

Along the way, Jason was cantor and soloist for Saint Patrick's Cathedral and soloist for Temple Israel while living in New York City. His opera repertoire contained more than 25 major roles. He was leading baritone soloist with the Opera Company of Boston, the National Theatre of Yugoslavia in Zagreb and Split, the Wiesbaden Opera in West Germany, and in New York's Lyric Opera and Bel Canto Opera. He performed as guest soloist with several leading symphony orchestras, including the Atlanta Symphony, the Boston Symphony, the Greenville Symphony, the Long Beach Symphony and the National Repertory Orchestra.

In his musical roles with the theatre, Jason Byce starred with such notables as Shirley Jones in *Bitter Sweet*, Andrea McCardle in *Annie Get Your Gun*; Ruth Lee in *Unsinkable Molly Brown*; Elke Sommer in *Woman of the Year*; Lainie Kazan in *Funny Girl*; John Carradine in *The Fantastics*; Stella Parton in *Seven Brides for Seven Brothers*; Avery Schreiber in *A Funny Thing Happened on the Way to the Forum*; John Cullum in *Camelot*; John Astin in *Lend Me a Tenor*; and Cindy Williams in *Moon Over Buffalo*, to name a few.

Jason appeared on several daytime television series including *"All My Children," "Days of Our Lives," "One Life to Live"* and *"As the World Turns."* He also guest-starred on locally filmed shows, such as *"I'll Fly Away," "Savannah,"* and *"In the Heat Of the Night,"* starring Carroll O'Connor. He was recognized by a guest appearance on *"Live with Regis and Kathi Lee"* for his popular *Polaner All-Fruit* commercial, in which he delivered a line which became his famous mantra: *"Would you please pass the jelly?"* He said this to some haughty, high-brow dining guests who were, in turn, shocked at his question. This particular commercial was so popular that it ran for more than 16 years, and became one that inspired many comedians. I can still hear him saying things like that at Roswell Elementary and Roswell High School playing the clown and keeping us all in stitches! Jason told me he had made in the six figures with that particular sentence!! So much for dog food!!

"When I watch TV., I jump for joy while the *Polaner* Commercial is run. I eat it with pleasure and fun 'cause the 'Jelly-man' is my son!" wrote Bo. No mother loved her child anymore than this mother.

Locally, Jason starred in two productions at Theatre in the Square of *"Lend Me a Tenor"* (Tito Merelli) and *"Little Joe Monaghan"* (Fred Palmer) and directed the 1994 production of *"1940's Radio Hour."* He was presented the coveted "Jenny Award" as Best Actor for both of these performances. In July of 1996, as part of the Atlanta Cultural Olympics, Jason Performed a leading role with the Atlanta Opera in a staged concert performance of Gershwin's Pulitzer award-winning *"Of Thee I Sing."* For two seasons he also sang the narration for The Atlanta Youth Orchestra's Christmas Production of *"The Polar Express."*

In 1993, Ervin (Jason) again renewed his friendship with MaryEm Robinson West. Remember her—from cherub choir and First Baptist Atlanta when Bo was living there with her parents and Luke was in World War II? MaryEm's name was always in his address book.

50" On The Front ... Now, It's On To The Back-Nine!
(Ervin's Poem to Eddie on his 50th Birthday)

There's a Lot to be remembered when looking back through years and time.
I'm not sure how it all started, but it had a reason and a rhyme.
You know, good friends are hard to come by, especially nowadays;
But, *Best Friends* are truly special ... here, let me count the ways:

When you grow up by-your-lonesome, with no siblings by your side,
I guess it's only natural to want a "Brother" in whom to confide.
And if the gods are kind enough, that person comes along ...
Sharing stories, pains, abilities, warm friendship and a song.

Those early years of discovering life and it's vast plate of wonders
Were filled with trial and error ... mistakes, triumphs and blunders.
With wobbly knees, we emerged in the new knowledge we had found,
And the bond forged then grew stronger with every leap and bound.

The classroom could not subdue our inherent playful natures ...
The ratio of learning to horseplay was our teachers' worst fears.
But, *somehow* we both made the grade, tho' "conduct" was not all "A's".
Damn! We had some fun together in those dear, sweet, golden days!

Sports always played a really big part in cementing our rapport.
But wins and losses fade away when you read the final score:
An understanding and respect we shared on gridiron, court or track
Taught us to face our up's and down's, and never to look back.

Tho' rivals in our college years, our friendship, based on trust
Has seen those "Tiger Paws" and "Paladin Hoofs" vanish in the dust.
And the paths we chose to navigate have led through rain and woods;
Mine through chilly dressing rooms ... yours through frozen foods.

A god-send or plain good fortune, I thank my luck star
For the "Brother" I call "Eddie", who's been with me, near and far.
It's hard to believe that after fifty years, and all the miles we've gone,

When we're together, time stands still from those early seeds we'd sown.

Now, one last word for my *Best Friend*, and then I'm out the door.
—You always pop into my mind when someone's yellin' "FORE!!!!"—
The past five decades have been the best. Now that they're a part of Lore...
On the green links of life, with no handicap, Let's tee it up for fifty more!!

Ervin Luther Buice, Jr., Growing Up

"LETTER FROM A FRIEND"

Bill and Gail Ivey are life-long friends of Jason. Living in California, they are unable to be in attendance today, and ask that the following letter be shared with you.

The very best thing that happened to me while serving in the Army Medical Service Corp was meeting my friend, Jason Byce.

We met in the summer of 1966 at Brook Army Medical Center in San Antonio, Texas during basic training. We both had received direct commissions as second lieutenants from the then President of the United States, Lyndon B. Johnson. We ended up becoming medical supply officers and accepting a host of other responsibilities to boot. Neither one of us wanted to be there, be we made the most of it. We especially had a lot of fun and laughter at the local army pub after class. It was there I learned how talented Jason was in voice and dance.

Soon after graduation, I was sent to the 94th Evacuation Hospital at Fort Lewis, Washington and I cannot recall where Jason was assigned. All I know is that Jason was sent to Viet Nam to join the 2nd Surgical Hospital about six months earlier than me. Shortly before departing for Viet Nam I was reassigned to the 27th Surgical Hospital.

Our troop ship arrived in Da Nang harbor around midnight, March 1968 at the beginning of the Tet Offensive. As the advanced party, I was in charge of taking the ready essential supplies loaded in two large containers on a barge to Chu Lai, about 50 miles south of Da Nang, along the China coast. The lost party happened to be the 2nd Surgical Hospital.

As we approached the harbor in Chu Lai, I radioed our host to make arrangements to be picked up and can you imagine that Jason answered the radio call to welcome me to Chu Lai! Our conversation continued for several minutes as we broke all the communication codes and rules of conduct. The Viet Cong that were listening must have thought we were crazy, but nevertheless I was relieved that my buddy was there to greet me.

ON ERVIN AND FRIENDSHIP

The time we spent in Viet Nam was extremely stressful, but the saving grace was our friendship and Jason's incredible ability to use humor under the most difficult of circumstances. We spent many evenings together at the Mag 12 Marine Air Base Officers Club. They had the best officer's club on the American Base Camp, although the target of many rocket attacks. In addition to playing games, such as The Lift and Aircraft Carrier Landings, Jason would sing opera and other popular songs. One evening while Jason was singing the Star Spangle Banner, the rockets started to fall all around us. At that point, Jason jumped on top of the bar, turned the background music to high volume and continued to sing while the rest of us headed for the bunkers. He became famous that evening. That's for sure!

Just before returning home, the 2nd Surgical Hospital was transferred to a location north of Saigon. I had not heard from Jason or knew of his whereabouts for several years after the war. Then out of nowhere we received a call from Jason. He was always great about keeping in touch with us and our friendship continued to foster as we kept in touch, frequently.

When Jason arrived in California to pursue his musical and acting career, we watched him perform in many theaters. We took our children, Taylor and Christina, to watch him perform as the Red Shadow. They will always remember Jason as the Red Shadow. He was just wonderful to our children. We saw him in *"Annie Get Your Gun, The Fantastics,"* and *"A Funny Thing Happened on the Way to the Forum,"* to mention a few. His television commercials were also hits. When we could, we enjoyed playing golf together and having him over to our home for dinner in Tustin, California.

My family will always fondly remember Jason. Jason sang at my father's funeral and spent many special evenings with our family. His happiest moments were when he reunited with MaryEm, his high school sweetheart and the enjoyment of her family. His humor, laughter, kindness and friendship will always be in our hearts.

Last summer MaryEm, Jason, Gail and I had the most delightful visit in Atlanta and we are so grateful we had that time together. I will indeed miss my army buddy and cherish the fond memories we will continue to share forever.

Love,

Bill and Gail Ivey

Bill & Gail Ivey, (Ervin's friend he met in VietNam),
MaryEm & Jason

#83 Bulloch Avenue, Roswell, Georgia,
Luke, Bo & Ervin's Home

Ervin with Suzie Donehoo, on a trip to Cherokee, N.C.

Ervin on his 9th Birthday, "showing off"

Ervin Buice & Linda Mansell, RHS Senior Superlatives, Most Versatile, 1962

1962 RHS Annual Staff Photo:
back(l-r): Dwight Rabern, Joe McDonald (deceased),
Terry Smith, Barry Mansell & Eddie Sullivan
front row: (l-r) Sue Johnson, Grace Stephens, Ervin Buice,
Editor, Linda Mansell, and Emily Ann Gentry

REST ASSURED

by
DONALD PAYTON

Senior Play

ROSWELL HIGH SCHOOL AUDITORIUM
FRIDAY, APRIL 13, 1962
8 o'clock

Directed by L. J. Isoman

CHARACTERS

Phillip Ulysses Morlock	Ervin Buice
Hazel Morlock	Bonnie Barron
Mary Morlock	Emily Ann Gentry
Jessica Morlock	Helen McLendon
Mildred	Eurelia Burtz
Joe Lanconi	Richard Reeves
Luigi Lanconi	Evelyn Jones
Martha Lanconi	Grace Stephens
Lucifer	Peggy Lynne Oliver
Liz Akers	Brenda Bowen
George Plew	Jerry Standridge
Mrs. Schmaltz	Mary Len Coker
Dr. L. B. Brown	Merrill Ruskin
Mr. Black	Terry Cornett
Jake	Lamar Strickland
Mrs. Frinck	Laura Morgan

PLACE: Living Room in the Morlock Home.

THE TIME

Act One: An evening of the present.
Act Two: Scene 1: An hour or so later.
Scene 2: The next day.
Act Three: The next day.

RHS Senior Class Play, in which Ervin Buice Began
his acting career, playing the lead role

Rev. Brantley Seymour, Linda Mansell marries
H. Alan Martin, June 6, 1964, the first couple to
be married in the new sanctuary

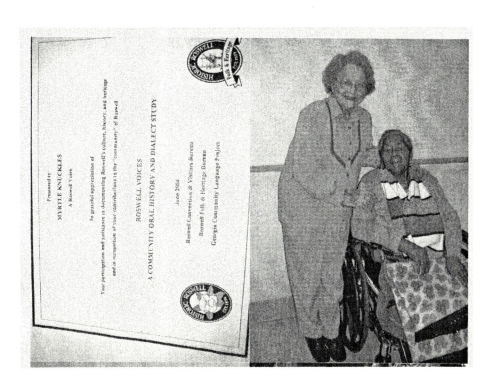

Bo with Myrt Knuckles, her long-time friend

Mr. Sargent's 7th Grade Class, 1956-57,
(Find Ervin, Linda, and others)

Jason (Erv), MaryEm, Ben, Allison, Shirley Jones, Luke, Bo

Jason & MaryEm's Wedding Photo—April 2, 1992

Jason and MaryEm's Love Song

As mentioned earlier, Ervin married Judi Fredericks in August of 1966 after their graduations from Furman University. MaryEm Robinson, in her senior year at West Georgia College, was introduced to John West, newly appointed Baseball Coach and Physical Education teacher there. They dated, fell in love and married in June of 1966.

MaryEm and Ervin had been friends since the age of three when they stood next to each other while singing in the Cherub Choir at First Baptist Church of Atlanta. During their teen years a beautiful friendship evolved as they both loved and shared many hours bowling, singing duets on voice recitals, Sunday afternoons at the Grant Park Zoo (Ervin loved animals) and water skiing at Lake Lanier or Allatoona. Ray and Virginia Smathers (lovingly known as "Papa and GinGin"), Minister of Music and Organist respectively, at First Baptist Atlanta, frequently invited voice students, Ervin and MaryEm, to accompany them for a day of fun in the sun, picniking and skiing. On one such occasion an entire afternoon was spent with MaryEm and Ervin attempting to recreate a Cyprus Gardens Florida Water Show. While skiing double, MaryEm made countless attempts to drop her skis while stepping on Ervin's knee in route to his shoulders where the ultimate pose would be made . . . it never happened! But, it was sure fun trying and they laughed about it for years.

Ervin would often mention his Roswell friends during conversations with MaryEm. Years later MaryEm so enjoyed finally meeting Merrill Rushin, Linda Mansell and Eddie Sullivan!

Though Ervin and MaryEm both dated others and had special "going steady" relationships while in high school they never allowed that to get in the way of their friendship. In his senior year at Roswell High School, due to a recent break-up up with his steady girlfriend, Ervin found himself without a date for the Jr/Sr Prom. So, with just one week left before the dance, Ervin felt comfortable in calling MaryEm to ask her for a date to the event. Sadly, it wasn't meant to be since MaryEm was "going steady" at the time. But, she wished she hadn't been! At the end of the summer of 1962, as Ervin and MaryEm prepared to leave for their respective colleges, they celebrated the occasion at their favorite Pizza place in Buckhead followed by strolling, hand in hand, the warm city streets (they were safe then) of Ansley Park . . . talking and laughing for hours before saying "good-bye". Years later, Bo showed MaryEm Ervin's first letter home from college, in which he wrote . . . "Say, Hello, to everyone for me, especially MaryEm". In the Fall of that same year Ervin invited MaryEm to be his date for the weekend of Furman's Homecoming. They double-dated with Ervin's roommate, Johnny Burrell and his girlfriend from back home. Who would have ever guessed that thirty-one year's later Johnny would be a guest at the wedding of Ervin and MaryEm? And, though the weekend of Homecoming had been a blast, it marked the close of a very special, sweet time in their lives. As they said their "good-byes" that brisk Fall Sunday afternoon they both felt a wistfulness knowing that they had come to a new juncture in their lives . . . a time to "grow up" and to grasp all of the joys, new friends and experiences that becoming a young adult would bring . . . But, at the same time holding on to the beautiful memories of their youth.

In 1967 MaryEm received a phone call from Mr. Smathers, who was now the Minister of Music at Briarcliff Baptist Church. He said that Ervin would be the guest soloist on the next Sunday Morning Worship Service since he would be leaving the following day for his deployment to Vietnam. MaryEm and John drove to Atlanta from Carrollton to hear Ervin sing, and to meet his wife Judi, on his last Sunday in America. "It was wonderful," MaryEm said. MaryEm remembers Ervin teasing her about her pregnancy. He could always make people laugh. Bo invited MaryEm and John to go out to eat with them following the service. That evening MaryEm prayed to God that He would watch over her precious friend and hold him in the palm of His hand while in battle . . . a prayer that would be repeated daily until Ervin was back, safely on American soil.

In 1976, Ervin wrote MaryEm a letter informing her of his and Judi's divorce. His demeanor was positive as he explained the reasons behind the mutual decision to end their marriage . . . they simply had grown apart as they both worked tirelessly in their chosen careers. He signed the letter, "Love, Jason". It seems that upon arriving in New York at the onset of his career he had been told of two changes that needed to be made. First, he must change his name since pronunciation recognition was a must in the field of entertainment. Hence we call him Jason! He also changed the spelling of Buice to Byce for the same reason. Secondly, he was told that he must "get rid of the Southern accent". In retrospect one might question this suggestion since that accent certainly came in handy when filming the commercial for Polaner All-Fruit which ran on TV for 16 years. We all take joy in remembering how he delivered that famous line, "Would ya please pass the jelly?" Jason's decision to change his name was, understandably, met with sadness by his parents. However, they along with everyone else wanting what was in his best interest to be the case, reluctantly accepted his new moniker. Of course, to those of us who had grown up with him "Erv" would always be "Erv"!

Ervin's career began to blossom and he was literally performing all over the world singing leading Operatic roles playing lead roles in musical theatre and filming soap operas and commercials while in New York. He starred in several Broadway Musicals, like *"Annie"* and TV's commercial, *"Frito Bandito."* When performing in Atlanta he would always leave comps at "will call" for MaryEm and John.

In April 1981, MaryEm's husband, John West, died suddenly of a massive heart attack. At the time of John's death they had three children . . . Allyson(12), John(8), and Jayson(6). (See Departures for the details) MaryEm continued to teach school, and was very active in her church: First Baptist of Powder Springs, and was totally involved in her children's lives. God led them through the valley and used her family in a singing ministry which showed God's strength and provision.

As mentioned before, in 1984 Jason married Jada Corbett, a Flight Attendant, which union did not last but a couple of years due to incapability. Bo said, "This marriage was a real mistake—but hopefully our family made a good impression on Jada from the kind words she wrote to me."

The next time MaryEm heard from Jason was in 1991, when he was in Atlanta doing *"A Funny Thing Happened On the Way To The Forum"* at the Fox Theater. Jason, like his mother before him, never threw away an address book, and he, also like her, kept up with people. The name "MaryEm" was always in his address books, almost as if they were destined to be together. Wanting to get in touch with MaryEm, Jason pulled out the Atlanta phone book to verify MaryEm's number. To his surprise he found her name listed alone and showing a move to Marietta.

The weekend of June 14, 1991 found MaryEm and her son Jayson on a college trip to Charleston, South Carolina to visit The Citadel. While there MaryEm called home just to touch base with daughter Allyson who, as it turned out, had some very interesting news for her Mom. Allyson told her Mom that someone named "Jason Byce" had called her, and "he was very pushy!" Allyson, on the one hand, was not in the habit of giving out any information to a stranger over the phone while on the other hand, Jason, not accustomed to taking "no" for an answer in situations such as this, was determined to find out the 7specifics of just how he could get in touch with MaryEm. They hung up with his finding out *only* that she was expected to return home late on Sunday evening. Jason called again on Monday, fortunately for him this time speaking with twenty year old son, John. Knowing how excited his Mom had been to hear about the 'missed phone call" he immediately gave Jason the phone number at which he could reach his Mom.

June 18th, one day after his 47th birthday, Jason reached MaryEm by phone at Rich's Cobb Center where she was a part-time employee. The entire sportswear department was excited as a date was made for later that evening after work. Jason was 45 minutes late in his arrival at the Rich's parking lot as a result of using a friend's directions rather than the ones given to him by MaryEm. When he drove up, he jumped out of the car, threw both hands in the air and said, "Where in the hell am I?" He then leaned over to give MaryEm a quick "hello kiss" and cracked his head on the car door. MaryEm thought to herself, "he is back, my cherished friend, who always makes me laugh!"

They spent the next three hours in a booth at Casa Galardo catching up on the past ten years of their lives. Later that evening as Jason walked MaryEm to her car they found themselves in each other's arms, frozen in an embrace that brought back to them the love of their youth and the realization that, 'Ervin' had **finally** come home!

That summer Jason and MaryEm had a whirlwind courtship . . . both feeling seventeen again and "in love". By August they had scratched out a weekend to visit Eddie and Beverly Sullivan at their home in Perry, Georgia. That weekend, as well as many to come, was filled with golf for the guys and shopping for the girls, joke telling, the beautiful blending of Jason and Eddie's voices as they harmonized to old, beloved gospel hymns, and uproarious laughter at the continuous antics of those two. MaryEm found herself thinking about their high school teachers . . . what a handful this duo must have been! By summer's end it was clear to Jason that though he had traveled the world over he had "finally found true happiness in his own backyard".

In September he returned to California to pack up his belongings for the move back to his beloved Georgia. While there he wrote the following letter to MaryEm:

> Dear Baby of Mine,
> I just got off the phone with you tonight, and I feel like I know and love you more than ever. I can hardly wait to get back to hold you and love you, something that I've dreamed of for years. You mean so much to me. You make me feel good about myself, like I am worthy of who I am and what I've achieved, like I have finally found happiness with the woman I've always loved. It doesn't matter that you never made it on my shoulders with Ray and GinGin. You will always be on top with me. I can hardly wait to get back to Atlanta and you. You have given me a reason for pushing forward to whatever it is that lies ahead. I just hope that we can make the trip together. Okay? Know that you can

share with me anything at all and I feel that way with you. You mean so much to me. My words will probably never be able to express, but in my feeble way, I will give it my best shot.

With all my heart,
Jason

Jason and MaryEm were mindful not to allow the euphoria they were both feeling to plunge them into a premature decision to marry, but rather spent the next two years getting to know each other as the adults that they had become and at the same time weaving every aspect of their lives into 'one'. In reference to a past relationship of his, Jason pled with MaryEm, "Please don't let the **worst** part of my life ruin the **best** part of my life". Out of her deep love for him, MaryEm grew to truly understand Jason and found that it was amazing how 'alike' they were on a psychological and emotional level. She respected him and his phenomenal talent, always supporting him and taking pride with him in his achievements. Once, as MaryEm lay gravely ill at Piedmont Hospital with, as yet, an undiagnosed perforated bladder, she insisted that Jason not cancel his engagement to sing that night at a Furman Alumni Banquet in Atlanta. She knew that his primary joy in life came from singing and often joked that she knew she came second to music which was first place in Jason's life. Music was the common **thread** that had first brought them together and through the years had woven their hearts together, ultimately creating a loving masterpiece of two souls becoming one. They sang together at Church, weddings, banquets, he taught in her Music Classroom and directed the spring musical each year, attended college fraternity parties, high school football and baseball games, and learned how to change a diaper. They became a beloved part of each other's family.

One special evening, while vacationing in Florida with Buice family friends, Jason pulled MaryEm aside wanting to share with her a beautiful love song sung by the Kings Singers. He looked into her eyes, tears flowing down his cheeks, and said, "this is exactly how I feel about you!" Later he would sing this song, "A Red, Red Rose" to her at their marriage ceremony:

For my dear, sweet MaryEm, who fills my heart . . .

A RED, RED ROSE

O my Luve's like a red, red rose
That's newly sprung in June:
O my Luve's like the melodie
That's sweetly play'd in tune!

As fair art thou, my bonnie lass,
So deep in luve am I:
And I will luve thee still, my dear,
Till a' the seas gang dry:

Till a' the seas gang dry, my dear,
And the rocks melt wi' the sun;
I will luve thee still, my dear,
While the sands o' life shall run.

And fare thee weel, my only Luve,
And fare thee weel a while!
And I will come again, my Luve,
Tho' it were ten thousand mile.

—Robert Burns

I love you, Jason

July 4, 1992

It was during the blizzard of 1993, separated by twenty miles of icy roads, that Jason and MaryEm spent the day on the phone planning their wedding. On April 2, 1993, surrounded by immediate families and fifty close friends, MaryEm West married Jason Byce (ne: Luther Ervin Buice, II). The music for the occasion had been specially chosen by Jason, with each piece having deep meaning for the couple. Jason really "felt" the beauty of music and poetry, something he had learned as a young boy from parents who acknowledged the importance of the arts in one's life and dedicated themselves to exposing their son to the arts on every level. Jason, totally expecting the guests to sit quietly listening to the music, was somewhat "miffed" at all of the chit chat. However, his consternation soon evaporated into the lovely sounds of Vivaldi's **"Spring,"** announcing the entrance of Hannah (3 year old reluctant flower girl) and Benjamin (4 year old ring-bearer) and finally, on the arm of her son John, his "Sweet One", MaryEm. Reverend Larry Adams, dear Buice family friend, performed the ceremony. John's words at the ceremony brought tears to the eyes of his Mom and Jason, as he said, "Jason, it is in this ceremony that we give you **'our all'** . . . **our Mother**, and that we accept **you** as Husband to our Mother, Father to Allyson, Jayson and me, and

Grandfather to Benjamin and Hannah. We love you and welcome you into our family." And so it was, that in marrying MaryEm, Jason married a family, and they each one embraced him. His laughter was infectious, his joy spontaneous and his love for life and quest for happiness had, in his words "finally come full circle" and found free reign.

The next ten years were filled with such fun and happiness as MaryEm joined Jason in his travels to California, Canada, New York and other major cities of the U.S. as he continued to perform in some of Broadway's most loved musicals. The children were filled with pride watching Jason's performances in California, Canada, and in their own hometown, Marietta, Georgia. Once, Allyson and Jayson, with Benjamin and Hannah in tow **drove** to Toronto, Ontario to catch Jason's performance in *"Lend Me A Tenor."* It was Jason's birthday which made the visit even more special. They all celebrated his day with a trip to nearby Niagara Falls and that evening were treated to a surprise birthday dinner in the Hotel Restaurant with Jason's favorite foods, including bouillabaisse, being prepared by the head Chef.

Jason became a vital part of MaryEm's Choral Music program at Smitha Middle School and the students loved him, especially the eighth grade boys who looked forward to the days when "Mr. B" would be there to work with them on their "changing voices". Working together they took students on performance trips to Washington, D.C., Disney World, and cruises to The Bahamas. For two Christmas Seasons, Jason and MaryEm performed at Symphony Hall with The Atlanta Youth Orchestra, under the direction of Maestro Jere Flint, in eight performances *The Polar Express* . . . Jason as the singing narrator and MaryEm as the director or the on-stage children's choir, her Smitha choral students.

There were high school, college, and law school graduations and The Byce's saw their family grow with Jayson's marriage to Marianne Brooks and John's marriage to Lee Blanton. And then, of course, there were more grandchildren; Anne Hollins and Pate Charles to Jayson and Marianne and John "Jack" Riley to John and Lee. With each addition came added joy!

Being able to spend valuable time with Bo and Luke was high on Jason and MaryEm's list, while they, in turn, were so very happy to have their "baby" back home. The four of them enjoyed trips to yearly Buice Family Reunions in Forsyth County, Pigeon Forge, The North Georgia Mountains, to Indiana for the college graduation of Jason's god child, Kimsley Ferrar and Nashville, Tennessee to hear The Kings Singers in concert. They also decided to join the church in which Jason had grown up, Roswell First Baptist, and consequently became members of The Bo Buice Sunday School Class. Worshiping together enriched their lives and at the same time added the opportunity for more shared experiences in church related activities. (thanks to MaryEm Byce for this chapter)

Article from the Atlanta Journal and Constitution announcing Ervin (Jason) & MaryEm's Wedding

THANKSGIVING 1993! Photo Left to Right: Hannah Cybul, Allyson West Cybul, Benjamin Cybul, Jayson West, Bo & Luke Buice (Jason's parents), (above) Captain & John West, Clarice Whitener (Bo's sister Aunt Cat), MaryEm & Jason.

Jason & MaryEm's New Family Photo

Jason gives MaryEm a Suprise Birthday Party!

MaryEm & Jason, Beverly & Eddie Sullivan, 1994

Bo Buice, the 5th Grade School Teacher, 1960

Bo, The School Teacher

By way of review, Bo taught two years at Duluth High School following her graduation from the University of Georgia in 1937. In 1939 Luke and Bo married and lived in Winder. Bo taught Junior High in Winder. As Luke got promotions, they moved. Next, she taught 6th and 7th grades in Sandersville, Georgia. Then they moved to Walterboro, South Carolina where she worked in the office of the hotel there where they lived. It was while they were in Walterboro that Luke was drafted into the service. From Walterboro, she came back home to live with her parents during the war.

When Luke was drafted into the service in 1942, he attended Harvard for about 6 months in Cambridge, Massachusetts for officer's training in the Navy. He rented a little apartment for Bo. He could only come to her on the weekends, but everything is so historic in that part of the United States, and because Bo's favorite subject was History (Social Studies) and English, they had such a good time touring places of historical interest, like Boston, Philadelphia, and others.

From Harvard, Luke was sent to San Diego, California, in preparation for being shipped to the South Pacific. Bo came with him, and while in San Diego, she was secretary at the Arden Farm Dairy. She remembers how kind the people were to her there. They gave her a baby shower prior to Ervin's birth. When she returned to Georgia and lived with her parents in Brookhaven, because Ervin was little and needed her, she didn't teach. When she moved to Roswell when Luke got home from the war, she began teaching again (1948).

Roswell Elementary and Roswell High School were in the same building in the 50's on Mimosa Boulevard. Mr. Walter Adams was the Principal. He discovered that Bo was a teacher through Mary and Aubrey Hawkins, members of Roswell First Baptist Church, with Bo and Luke. Mr. Adams asked Bo to come and teach the seventh grade, which she taught for the next five years. She resigned to have surgery the summer of 1951. Later she was called back to teach by W. J. Dolvin, the Principal of the elementary school, who just happened to be Bo and Luke's neighbor. W. J. and Emily Dolvin, former President Carter's Aunt Sissy, lived at the end of Bulloch Avenue. Bo remembers Dolvin walking up to their home one evening, and said he would give her the best grade in school if she would come back. She was offered the fifth grade, which she readily accepted and taught for the next 28 years!

Bo could also teach the Bible in school back then. She called it "Great Literature," which, of course, it is. She taught this first thing in the morning, and she had a "Socrates" chair. If a child was not paying attention, or was "acting up," he or she had to go and sit in this chair in the corner for awhile and "think." She had this sign high up on the wall, which read, "Think." She said that she had very little problem with discipline because she allowed them to do "fun" things in order to learn following the teaching on a subject. She said that she would let them get up occasionally and march around the room, and she would hit something, which was their signal to sit down wherever they were. Sometimes she would tell them to put their heads on their desks for a little rest and would play pretty music, just anything to give them a break. They sang a lot of songs, also, to keep them entertained. She read to her students interesting stories like "The Secret Garden."

Bo had to be careful about having "favorite" students. The girls always said she favored the boys, since she had a little boy, but she loved them all. It is hard to imagine, but back then parents would often request that their children be in certain teachers' rooms, and the classes would be set up accordingly by the teachers—it became a sort of "popularity contest," as the teacher would say, "This one is mine. The parent asked that I get this one."

Midge Williams, a fellow teacher of Bo's, who taught the seventh grade at Roswell Elementary, says that she believes Bo was popular with the children because they felt "safe" under her "nurturing" influence. When the children would line up in the mornings to bring Bo their lunch money, they would often "confide" to her personal and sometimes troubling things.

Bo was honored with teaching the first TAG (Talented and Gifted) students at Roswell Elementary. She taught some fifth and sixth graders Advanced English and Social Studies. She was selected by the Principal to assume this honorable responsibility.

Bo and Margaret Standard (Ovbey) met the Fall of 1962, the year Ervin started college at Furman University. Margaret, originally from Griffin, Georgia, was one of three new teachers at Roswell Elementary that year, and because she lived in Roswell, she became well-known as the "single" Special Education Teacher. Bo was teaching the fifth grade at that time. They became real good friends. When asked how long it took them to become friends, Margaret answered, "a couple of days." She was "compassionate" and Bo added, "nice," to which they both laughed. Margaret became like a daughter to Bo. She sort of "filled" that void when Ervin left home. "Letting go" is hard for most mothers because we pour so much into the lives of our children.

Margaret met Jim Ovbey, originally from Marietta, the second year she was in Roswell at a state convention for exceptional children. Jim was impressed by Margaret's new car. Margaret joined Bo and Luke over at Bob's Dairy Barn one evening, and she left early saying, "Jim is coming over." At the time, she was living with Dorcas and Hershel David on Mimosa Boulevard, not far from the Buice's. Bo commented that night about Jim: "He wears well," meaning they looked good together. She meant that Margaret needed him. Margaret and Jim were married in 1966 and first lived in a terrace apartment on Thomas Circle across the street from Bob and Mary Alice Campbell and Helen and Tim Combs. Jim was a school principal.

Today Margaret and Jim Ovbey are the proud parents of two grown sons, Tim, who teaches first grade in the Atlanta school system and Joe, who is in New York, trying to get into show business, following in Ervin's footsteps. Jim, now retired, won the award for the best honey in Georgia. Margaret, also retired, is still a close friend of Bo's, running by several times a week to check on her. It is a friendship that has spanned a long time. Like Bo, Margaret also graduated from the University of Georgia, and they both have a great sense of humor and enjoy "teasing" one another.

When Luke moved into his store on Canton Street, Margaret remembers painting the baseboards lying down on the floor. She did many things for and with Bo and Luke; they filled a void in her life as well. Margaret said, "She was my mother away from my mother." Margaret's mother lived in Griffin, and at times became a little jealous of her and Bo's close relationship, but Margaret assured her, "Mom, you are loved for accepting me for who I am—and not for what you want me to be." Margaret wrote Bo, "Destiny shaped my life, but it took your helping hand to smooth off the rough edges."

Bo was presented "The Lifetime PTA Membership Award" for longevity and professionalism when she retired by the Principal's Advisory Committee. Bo retired from teaching public school in 1980, when she was 65 years old, but she continued teaching Sunday School well into her 80's. There was a reunion in 1987 of the teachers. Bo wrote an "Ode" to all the individual teachers. Bo is still teaching. Teachers teach. She's teaching me. She's teaching you through me. Bo Buice continues to make a difference in many lives.

Author Unknown:

> The dinner guests were sitting around the table discussing life. One man, a CEO, decided to explain the problem with education. He argued, "What's a kid going to learn from someone who decided his

best option in life was to become a teacher?" He reminded the other dinner guests what they say about teachers: "Those who can, do. Those who can't, teach." To stress his point he said to another guest; "Susan, you're a teacher, be honest. What do you make?"

Susan, who had a reputation for honesty and frankness replied, "You want to know what I make? I make kids work harder than they ever thought they could. I make a C+ feel like the winner of the Congressional Medal of Honor. I make kids sit through 40 minutes of study hall in absolute silence. You want to know what I make? I make kids wonder. I make them question. I make them criticize. I make them apologize and mean it. I make them write. I make them read, read, read. I make them show all their work in math and perfect their final drafts in English. I make them understand that if you have the brains, and follow your heart, and if someone ever tries to judge you by what you make, you must pay no attention because they just didn't learn." Susan paused and then continued. "You want to know what I make? I MAKE A DIFFERENCE. What do you make?"

"I remember the time I didn't do my homework and Mrs. Buice made me stay after school and do it. I was supposed to walk home that day (I walked home every day) and go to my grandmother's house (Ellen Coleman) because my mother was not going to be home. When I found out I was going to have to stay after school, I told Mrs. Buice that I could not because I had to go to my grandmother's house and she would be expecting me and she would worry if I didn't show up.

Well, Mrs. Buice said, "You just march yourself down to Mr. Dolvin's office and tell Mrs. Howell that you need to use the telephone to call your grandmother and tell her that you are going to be late."

And so, I burst into tears and remember walking down the hall so embarrassed. Mrs. Buice taught me a lesson that day and that was . . . 'You don't fool around with Mrs. Buice!'"

Hal Coleman

Roswell Elementary & High School (erected 1914, closed 1990); Roswell Elementary, 1949, the year Bo started teaching there. (The High School & Elementary were combined from 1949-53)

Faculty (l-r) top row: Mrs. Dorothy Walker, Mrs. Marie Martin, Mrs. Sarah Hughes, Miss Broadwell, Mrs. Bo Buice, Mrs. Chessie Rucker, Mrs. Dorothy Lowry, Mrs. Alda Lyons, Mrs. Holbrook, Mrs. Sybil Wells, Mr. Lucian Bell, Miss Parham, Mrs. Jackson, Mrs. Phillips, Sec.

Second row (l-r): Mrs. Cross, Mrs. Wing, ?, Mrs. Phillips, ? Mr. Charles Newton, Mrs. Donehoo, & Mr. Walter Adams, Principal

Bo's Fifth Grade Class, 1972-73, Roswell Elementary School

Row I (front)—Linda Price, Serita Nicholson, Mike Graham, Tammy Vickery, Cleo Koller

Row II—Stead Mixson, Jan Whiteman, Greg Horner, Lisa Roberts, Sammy Pittman, Lollie Threatt, Tim Connelly and Mrs. Bo Buice

Row III—Scott Sullivan, Susan Smith, Jim England, John Marlow, Robin Turner, Jeff Ethridge

Row IV—Phyllis Langley, Scott Bannister, Joy Floyd, Linda Hill, Kathy Kennedy, Jimbo Mabry & Charlene Holm

RETIREMENT OF JASPER DOLVIN, CHESSIE RUCKER AND SYBIL WELLS
(June, 1966)

To Chessie Rucker:

Chessie Rucker, how we'll miss you,
As your good deeds we review!
Your punctual way, your loyal support,
Your skill in handling the book report.
We'll await September midst fear and gloom,
As mamas want Johnny "in Mrs. Rucker's room!"

To Sybil Wells:

Sybil Wells, we'll miss you, too!
You've walked with grace and honor true.
Parents and children, and teachers agree
You're a professional, sincere as can be.
It's teachers like you our children need.
Norcross is lucky to have you, indeed!

To Mr. Dolvin:

Mr. Dolvin, the time has now come
To express our regard and say well done!
Your spirit will linger in every space;
A big man like you just can't be replaced!
We'll remember your kindness, you wit, and your charm,
And urge every teacher to subscribe to "State Farm."
Your friends wish you luck and hearty cheers
For health and long life in retirement years!

(Addendum):

To Margaret Standard Ovbey (bride to be):

Margaret Standard, our July bride,
To all of your talents we look with pride.
The days would be dull and rather limp
If it were not for you, our faculty imp!
Each grade would be orderly, but fill with gloom
Without you popping into every room.
We give you to Jim and wish for you two
The best things in life and happiness true.

                    --Bo Buice

Bo-Bo,
It took me a <u>minute</u> to realize that you were a special person, an <u>hour</u> to appreciate you, a <u>day</u> to love you, but it would take an <u>entire</u> <u>lifetime</u> to forget you!
I <u>truly</u> love you,
Margaret
October 20, 2005

Margaret & Jim Ovbey; The Ovbey's and Ervin

Roswell First Baptist Church, Roswell, Georgia
This Sanctuary erected in 1964

The Church in the Buice's Life

Roswell First Baptist Church began in 1872 with 22 members, meeting in a building near the old Roswell Department Store (now, Public House). Most were mill workers, and they met in homes until 1875.

In 1910, Reverend Ralph Donehoo became the Pastor of Roswell First Baptist. He resigned and moved away in 1912. Rev. Mercer Williams replaced him. His ministry ended on a Sunday in 1915, the year Bo was born. He started to church in a buggy and when he reached Hog Waller Creek, it was flooded. As he tried to cross, he was tragically drowned. The church recalled Rev. Donehoo, who served from 1916 until 1935. He married my parents, Joe Mansell and Lessie Coleman Mansell in October of 1928. Rev. Donehoo's salary was $8.60 for preaching two Sundays a month.

At that time, the church was where Second Baptist Church stands today. A group of members wanted the church to move to a more central location, so they bought property on Main Street (now Mimosa Boulevard), and built a new sanctuary for $1,000, which is now our chapel, named for Rev. Donehoo. But wouldn't you know, as happens in many churches, there was a split over moving. The majority moved to our present site, and the others stayed and organized the Second Baptist Church, and this group kept the piano.

The members paid Rev. Donehoo $5.00 each to purchase pews for the new sanctuary, which he had the machinery to make, with some people donating the timber.

In 1935, when Rev. Donehoo retired, RFBC asked him to help them find a new pastor, so he contacted the President of Mercer University, who recommended R. Lee Buice, older brother of Luke Buice. Lee Buice became the first full-time pastor of RFBC. (Another squabble erupted because some members didn't want to meet every Sunday!) But Lee Buice is believed to have baptized the largest number of people at one time in the history of the church!! Following one revival, he baptized over 40 people. He served from 1935 until 1943. The church built a pastorium during his tenure. Both Rev. Donehoo and Rev. Buice were also school principals while pastoring.

Roswell First Baptist was without a Pastor when Luke and Bo first came to Roswell in 1948. Bo and Luke were very influencial in bringing Brantley Seymour to Roswell in 1949. He served the church for 34 years, under whose leadership, the church grew. The Donehoo chapel was remodeled, and the Sanctuary and Educational Annex were dedicated in 1964. (As I said once before, Alan and I were the first couple married in the new sanctuary June 6, 1964). The church elected its first secretary, Mrs. Hilda Moore, the first Minister of Education, Ralph Crawford, the first Minister of Music, Don Snell and a Minister of Youth, Nancy Burch.

Once when Luke got sick, Bo was running around trying to get everything together to take him to the hospital, Brantley came to her rescue and went across the street to The Roswell Department Store (owned by my father, Joe Mansell and Ben Tolbert) and purchased some new pajamas for Luke. Bo commented, "Brantley was a real pastor, a friend to everyone," to which I readily concurred, remembering how kind and caring he always was to our family as well.

Bo saved a letter written to her and Luke from Brantley, dated July 2, 1956. Ervin would have been 12 at the time.

> Dear Luke and Bo,
> I wanted to thank you for helping me carry the boys to Camp Pinnecle. You were so kind.
> Bo, I wanted to thank you for working in Vacation Bible School.
> You have every reason to be proud, as I know you are, of Ervin. He was an outstanding camper.
> It is nice to have friends.!! God bless you and yours.
>
> Sincerely,
> Brantley

Bo saves poetry and important periodicals, just as I do and here is one we both love concerning the church:

"About 100 years ago, Alexis de Tocqueville, French politician and writer, visited America, and wrote a book about the people he learned to know so well. Among other things, he said this:

"I sought for the greatness and genius of America in her commodious harbors and her ample rivers, and it was not there; in her fertile fields and boundless prairies, and it was not there. Not until I went to the churches of America and heard her pulpits aflame with righteousness did I understand the secret of her genius and power. America is great because she is good, and if America ever ceases to be good, she will cease to be great."

Oh, America, America, God shed His grace on thee!! "In God we still trust," is my prayer!

One such article from Bo's collection from *The Atlanta Journal Constitution*, dated December 25, 1960, entitled "God's Love Preached; But Hate Practiced," by Harold Martin. (Different from my husband who is also Harold Alan Martin) Sadly, things haven't improved since that time:

> "From wherever heaven is, O God, look down upon us in mercy and compassion on this the birthday of Your Son. You sent Him, as a baby nearly 2,000 years ago, to tell us how to live in peace and love together on this earth.
>
> We heard His message, and for all that time we have been speaking of it to each other. It has been translated into every language, it has been carried into every far-off place. We have in truth gone into all the earth and preached the gentle gospel to every creature as we were told to do.
>
> But somehow, we have failed. We have preached love and practiced hate. We have preached brotherhood, but we have withdrawn in revulsion from the practice of brotherhood.
>
> We have been profligate with our words and stingy with our actions. You have shown us the way of light. We have preferred to walk in the shadows of selfishness.
>
> You have asked us to follow the high, straight road of sacrifice. We have preferred to wander in the lowlands, chasing the will-o-the wisp of material comforts.
>
> You have asked us to fix our hearts and minds on things of the spirit. We have fixed them instead on the things of the world. We have allowed our souls to become so gnarled and knotted that we have lost contact with Thee, and with Thy Son.
>
> We will feel the loss today, when we go to church, and kneel to pray. Our words will falter as we try, like troubled children, lost and frightened, to find our way back to our Father and His love again.
>
> Please, Lord, hear these stumbling prayers, and forgive us, as down all the centuries You have so graciously forgiven all our faults and failures. For so long as we do remember the birthday of

Your Son—so long as we even try to comprehend the message of love and gentleness He brought to the world, there is still hope for us. Amen"

Look for strength in people, not weakness; for good, not evil. Most of us find what we search for.

—Wilbur Chapman

Bo Buice loves the Church and the Lord of the Church as much as anyone I ever met. She is so dedicated to the Lord's Body in the earth. She invites everyone she meets to Church. What if we all did that? What a different world it would be. Bo has a burden for people who have never tried the Church, or who've tried it and have left, for whatever reason, to come back. After all, if we can't get along with God's people on earth, how can we expect to go to heaven, and live with God's people there forever? C. S. Lewis once said that if we live for the life to come we will get this one in the deal. But if we live only for this life, we will lose both! Think about that.

The Bible teaches that the church is Jesus' Body in the earth. We are all needed to be part of His Body, to make a difference in our little corner of the world, to grow up and to be accountable. No man is an island unto himself. We are all in community for a reason: we need each other!! I know sometimes other people hurt us and offend us and make us cry. But they also build us up, help us, hold us to a higher plane of life. That is why Christians are called "His Body." (Eph. 1:22, 23). We all need one another. The hand needs the arm and the shoulder and the trunk. Jesus is the head, and all of us are his different parts. We are here to see each other through—not to see through each other.

When I asked Bo how does a Christian keep from being a Pharisee, she replied, "I've learned to wait about sizing people up. We don't know the background of others. We don't know what they've been through. We need to think deeper. We need to size ourselves down before we size others up!!" When working with children, she said that we are to, "First, come down to their level—we shouldn't expect them to come up to our's." How true!

The Church is our most important family—the one with which we will spend eternity. We need to love the church and "let the Church guide our lives," as Pope Benedict XVI told the one million youth gathered at World Youth Day in Cologne, Germany on Sunday August 21, 2005. He urged the people gathered there to be guided by church doctrine as they exercise freedom, and to realize that "religion constructed on a 'do-it-yourself' basis cannot ultimately help us." He went on to say, "There is no room for apathy and disengagement, and even less for partiality and sectarianism." Jesus taught His followers that "the gates of hell shall not prevail against the Church."(Matt. 16:18) He was talking about the universal Church—not your church or my church, but His Body in the World, The Church.

No, the church isn't perfect because it is made up of imperfect people. It is in reality a place where people should go to be accepted, loved, taught, healed, equipped, forgiven, encouraged, and sent out to reach others. As someone once said, "The Church is not made up of perfect people but of 'forgiven' people." It is like a hospital for hurting people, not a place where people go to get hurt!

Bo wrote a paper and made a talk on "Are We the Body of Christ? These are the highlights of her talk:

> The Church has been a major part of my life. For many years I have studied and taught the scriptures. Study and experience have shown me how truly applicable God's word is to life.
>
> The lack of respect for life and moral breakdown in America should cause Christians in every church and denomination to ask, "Are we the body of Christ?"
>
> The scripture compares the church to the body of Christ. Christ desired to be with His followers always. When He returned to His Father, He promised that He would return to every believer in the form of the Holy Spirit. Those of us who receive Him and are baptized with His Spirit are His body: walking, talking and ministering in the world. We are the universal Church, taking His place in the individual churches.
>
> Does the world recognize Him in us? The human body is a divine miracle, the Temple of God. Properly cared for, it is a blessing to us and to others. It is a convincing comparison to Christ's body or to church members. Christ is the Spiritual Head, but the members are responsible for the care and function of the local body. The members have different gifts and responsibilities. Each should be used only to coordinate and strengthen the Body.
>
> The local *Head* is the church leadership, ministerial and lay. The Body will not function without proper leaders. They should have sound, well-trained minds whose whole purpose is to think like the spiritual head, and to be a guide to the body members. The strength of the leadership is shown in the cooperation and spirit of the body members.
>
> Let us make a comparison with some members of the church to Christ's Body. In Christ's Body the *Eyes* are necessary. Leaders and members need clear, well-rounded vision. Farsighted power to see future opportunities; near sight to see and correct mistakes—and peripheral vision to be aware of other's needs and to see both sides of all matters. Cataracts caused by sin will blind us, and limited vision will cause the body to stumble. Removal is possible.

The *Ears* should be tuned first to God's will, then to the opinions of others—not itching ears, but listening ears, deaf to whatever hinders the Body, but open to Truth.

The *Tongue* is the most abused member of the Body. The tongue should praise God and others, and measure its words. It should be much in prayer, tactfully disagree, and always comfort the needy. The tongue should not bear false witness, be a busy-body or a viper. It should never say to or about another member, words it would not want to receive itself.

The *Hands* are the useful body members. They should be strong, capable hands that lift. Hands that are good at work and at clean up. Christ has no hands but ours in the church today.

The *Feet* must go, prayerfully directed, where Christ leads—feet that are able to stand, ready to walk with others through life's joys and shadows, feet that avoid fault-finding missions.

Christ's body needs a *Great Heart*! It is the assistant to the sound mind—the body's guide to mature, Christ-like attitudes and actions, bearing no ill will. It should pump always for the well-being of the Body. If ill will is present, the scripture says we are to remove it and forgive. If we do not do so, God will not forgive us and will not answer our prayers. Neither will He accept our offering.

'The three middle letters of heart spell "ear;" the first four letters spell "hear." Can I hear with the ear in my heart? The last three letters spell "art." Is there an art to hearing with my heart?

He has put the ear in the center of the heart so we can hear Him. We have been trying to under-stand Him with the wrong set of ears. He wants us to hear Him on the inside. Everything God does inside of a person, He does it through the heart. I cannot fathom receiving wisdom from God without a wise and hearing heart.

Each member in the Body needs love, respect and support of the other members. Some may get a Headache, but many have a real heartache. If the Body of Christ suffers, the cause must be traced to source of the problem, and surgery may need to be performed. Diseases such as suspicion, hatred, ignorance, criticism, jealousy, personal grudge, desire for authority, unforgiveness, and/or indifference may be disabling the Body of Christ.

Christ wants no division in His Body. We must all be baptized with His Spirit. If not, we are not part of His Body. True members must hasten to call the Great Physician. He has the cure. We may need a Spiritual Physical and a Spiritual remedy. Then and only then can we really become the whole Body of Christ in the earth, enabling Him to walk, talk, and minister through us, wherever we go."

THE CHURCH IN THE BUICE'S LIFE

Some people quit going to Sunday School and church when Bo stopped teaching. This saddened her greatly. We go or don't stop going to church because of people like Bo. We go or should continue to go because the Lord Jesus instructed us to go and left us an example of going and assembling regularly with other believers! (see I John 2:19 & Hebrews 10:25) **What part are you in the Body? Are you the missing part?**

—

Bo started the first RA's—Royal Ambassadors in her home for Roswell First Baptist. She taught them from the scriptures, served refreshments, then let them go out to play. She was also Vacation Bible School Director one year. All these are now sweet memories.

My dear friend and sister in the Lord, Diane Dorris, from one of Bo's first Sunday School Classes at First Baptist Roswell remembers Mrs. Buice saying, "Girls, things won't always be as well with you as they are now." Bo said that she meant we should learn to enjoy every stage of life, no matter what happens, because each stage is different and each stage is trying. Diane wondered what she meant, but now that she is older, she understands completely what Bo was saying. Another class member, Margo Coleman, gave Diane and Johnny the address of Wilma and Calvin Sandlin, Missionaries to the Ute Indians in Utah, at a missions conference, "Christmas in August" at First Baptist in the summer of 1971. Due to not being able to have children naturally, Diane and Johnny were seeking God for children to adopt. In God's time, they became the proud parents of three American Indian children from Utah: Tim, Tina and Carmella. Today, they are the proud grandparents of eight beautiful grandchildren (and #9 on the way) and they all live in the Crabapple and Forsyth County areas. Thanks, Bo, for another indirect influence.

In 1979, Bo was approached by Rev. Seymour and the Education Minister, and asked if she was "game" to start a coed class, which she did in October of that year. Back then, Baptist Churches didn't have couples' classes. It was very rare for men and women to meet together. Bo commented, "Doesn't that sound like the 'Dark Ages' now?" She told them she'd be willing, and she had 98 on roll in three months in the "Bo Buice Class," which class is still going strong today although Bo is no longer the teacher but still a member. Some of the first couples were Wendell and Nancy Phillips, Pat and Sherry Moss, Saundra and N.D. Brumbeloe, Liz and J.W. Holloway, Helen and Tim Combs.

Saundra Brumbeloe, from the 60's class, is one of the few who started with Bo back in the beginning and is still in her class, along with her husband, N.D. I told her she deserves an award for "faithfulness." Norma Hawkins invited Saundra, so Norma deserves an award also. This is how the chain works.

Dr. Jerry A Songer came to RFBC on November 6, 1983. During his tenure, Primrose Cottage was bought and sold. The Gentry property was purchased for future growth and an educational annex was built. It was during his pastorate that Bo was ordained as the first female deacon, Oct. 4, 1987.

Dr. Ron Bradley, the present Pastor at Roswell First Baptist Church, whose first Sunday was November 1st, 1997, preached a sermon on January 8, 2006 entitled, "If I Weren't a Preacher, Why Would I Join a Church?" based on Matthew 16:13-18. In it he made some startling statements:

"Twenty three million so-call 'Christians' in America do not attend church on a regular basis. Ten million only attend on Christmas and Easter." This is a startling statistic. These "lone-ranger" Christians think they can make it through the year on just two spiritual snacks. They are actually what Dr. Bradley called "spiritual orphans." "The church is the instrument God has chosen for the battle—to take on the enemies off Christ." Amen. God doesn't have any other plan.

Too many people in America "think" they have God and don't need the Church, which is His Body in the earth. The church was instituted by God and He is the Head of the Church, and believers are "the Bride of Christ," making Jesus the Bride-groom.

It is very difficult to have a relationship with the Father and His Son apart from His Body. It's like decapitating the Head from the Body. If we are "married" to Him, then we will want to be with Him and His Body, attached, committed, bearing one another's burdens, encouraging, exhorting, teaching, counseling, helping, loving one another, holding one another accountable, just like any other army. We will desire to "OBEY MY SON, JESUS." Dr. Bradley proclaimed that "170,000 people per day in other nations are coming to Jesus for salvation." Wow, and we in America, are too busy and too affluent to be interested much anymore. The Church of Jesus Christ will triumph and be victorious—"the gates of Hell shall not prevail against her." We are the "called-out" people, living in a fragmented society. "Called-out" means that we are "called to" regular, on-going growth and training. We are only as strong as our weakest member. Jesus always obeyed His Father, even to the point of death on cruel cross. Submission was not a role He chose, but a response He willingly gave. Surely, we can do the same as His children.

To repeat what Bo said about not becoming a Pharisee, a religious leader, who is legalistic, harsh and overbearing on doctrine, but short on love:

"It is almost impossible not to become one. We must learn to look beyond the way people dress, act or speak, and see the good, for there is good in everyone. We must wait about sizing people up. We don't know their background, what they've been through. We need to think deeper. We need to size ourselves down before we size others up. I'm afraid this has turned many people away from the church."

Just going to church doesn't make one a Christian, not any more than standing in a garage makes one a car! There are many people who "go" to church, but are certainly not believers. They go for reasons such as social, for making business contacts or political impressions. Some go just to "pacify" their spouses or to see that their children are taught morality and ethics. Some go just to be seen. God knows who belongs to Him; we can fool people, but we can't fool God; His sheep hear His voice and He calls each one by name. He says we are His people and the sheep of His pasture, and that he leads us in and out to pasture, meaning he leads his own, knows them and they know Him intimately.

We must all learn from the victories and the mistakes of others, because none of us will live long enough to make all the victories and mistakes ourselves. If we don't learn from those who have gone before, we have to learn all the lessons all over again. That is why we should study the lives of people who have preceded us. Studying the lives of great people, especially great Christians, not only gives us encouragement and enlightenment, but it also teaches us what we should avoid, and what or Who we should embrace. A former Pastor taught me a long time ago, "Don't accept someone's philosophy until you look at his or her life."

> "The church gives people what they need; the theater gives them what they want."—Evangelist Billy Sunday

In conclusion, as the song goes:

Oh, may all who come behind us find us faithful,
May the fire of our devotion light their way;
May the footprints that we leave lead them to believe
And the lives we live inspire them to obey.
Oh, may all who come behind us find us faithful.
—Mohr

Those people in the Bible are examples to us of how to live and what to do and not do. They teach us if we are teachable. We need to study their lives so we can understand God's dealings with us.

> "Many have quarreled over religion who have never practiced it."—Benjamin Franklin

Bo Buice teaching the Sunday School Class named for her with Stan Shuford, playing the instrument he made

BO BUICE SUNDAY SCHOOL CLASS - ROSWELL FIRST BAPTIST CHURCH, 2005

Front row: Molly Earls, Saundra Brumbeloe, Liz Holloway, Martha McConnell; Aubrey Hawkins
Bo Buice, Sadie Hogue, Linda Muth, Candy White
Middle row: Mike Earls, N.D. Brumbeloe, Johnny McKenzie, Betty Swanson, Patsy Shuford,
Helen Combs, Karen Whaley, Nancy Stidham, Jane Bishop, Peggy Varnell
Rodney Hogue, Dick Holzapfel
Back row: Bob Swanson, Stan Shuford, Tim Combs, Marvin Whaley, Rodney Hogue, Jerry
Bishop, Al Jones

The Bo Buice Sunday School Class—2005

To My Wonderful Class:
This is a happy time of year
And love is everywhere—
On cards and notes, in tender looks.
It's even in the air!

Luke has my heart, I'm not forlorn
Our love is tried and true—
But at 9:45 on Sunday morn
My heart belongs to you!   Bo Buice 2/15/85

Luke & Bo on cruise in 1987
when she was elected Deacon

Bo, The Deacon

Jim Stewart, one of the fine men in First Baptist Church of Roswell, was on the Deacon Search Committee at Roswell First Baptist in 1989 when Dr. Jerry Songer was Pastor. Jim suggested Bo as a candidate for service as Deacon, to the horror of some and the approval of others. That was so unusual for a man to suggest a woman. The Assistant Pastor, Rev. Bo Prosser, and Joe Carl Johnson, an older gentlemen and former missionary, stood for Bo also. Luke and Bo were on a trip when the church voted, and she received more votes than the others who were on the ballot, plus many write-in votes.

There was opposition, of course, from within and without the church. Other area churches thought First Baptist Roswell was making a big mistake. At least one couple who Bo knows about left the church, but the mother and grandmother of the wife stayed. The grandmother told Bo when she went to visit her later, "Mrs. Buice, I think I would have made a good Deacon." Bo agreed with her, "Mrs. Griffin, you would have made a wonderful Deacon." She understood better than her grandchildren the significance of the issue, and Bo said this was very unusual. Bo commented that the spirit in the church was wonderful, and has been ever since. "Now there are such fine young women who are such wonderful Deacons, who realize that I led the way, and they are so sweet to me as a result. They're so thankful." In 2006, there are 22 women deacons at RFBC, two deceased, and 105 men deacons, both active and inactive. Karen Waley, one of them wrote Bo, "Thank you for paving the way for other women to serve." (According to the Visions Magazine of the Cooperative Baptist Fellowship of Georgia, June/July issue of 2005, Oakhurst Baptist Church of Decatur was the first CBFGA Church to ordain women deacons in 1974.)

How did Bo overcome some of the writings of Paul in the New Testament to "justify" her being able to become a Deacon? In one of Bo's teachings on "Women in Service," I found this quote: "Paul admitted that part of what he said was his own words" which is true. There is only one scripture which she quoted and stood on in her deacon speech: "There is neither Jew nor Greek, there is neither male nor female: for we are all one in Christ Jesus." (Galatians 3:28) She said, "I know Paul was an Apostle, but he was also a man, and he saw things in his generation. Women had no opportunities. Women all over the world were just like they are today in Iraq. The sadness of the conditions of women even today in parts of the world is just unbelievable. It was never Christ's intention for women to be 'second-class' citizens. He would never have called Mary Magdalene, Mary and Martha of Bethany and other women to follow Him if He had had any prejudice, and of course, it is impossible for Christ to have any partiality." "But the wisdom that is from above is first pure, then peaceable, gentle, and easy to be intreated, full of mercy and good fruits, without partiality and without hypocrisy," wrote Jesus' half brother James in his letter, 3:17. Bo went on to say, "If we are like Christ, we don't have prejudice."

Note this carefully please, how Paul wrote in I Timothy 2:12-15, "And, I do not permit a woman to teach or to have authority over a man, but to be in silence." (Bo said, "This was Paul's opinion. Isn't that awful, 'in silence'—people don't accept that. We have to consider the culture in which Paul wrote.") "For Adam was formed first, then Eve. And Adam was not deceived, but the woman being deceived fell into transgression." (Bo interjected, "He followed her—it was even. They both sinned. He didn't have to eat that apple!!!") Amen. The old "blame game." Eve blamed the serpent; Adam blamed Eve. The game is still going on today. Everyone is responsible for his or her own choices. **God is not to be blamed for human choice.** Our choices do determine our destiny. Bo says, "Choices are important. They lead to commitments. Commitments form lifestyles."

Adam was incomplete until God created Eve. She completed him. "God's purpose was for completion in His creation who were to relate to Him and each other. His purpose was twofold—provide physical life, and in the fullness of time, the woman would be the channel or instrument through which He would come into the world. Jesus, son of Mary, who was not even allowed to be included in the census, did not put her on a throne but in acknowledging her as His mother, He gave all of us a level status in His spiritual family when He said, "Anyone who does the will of My Father is My mother, My brother and My sister." He created us all equal but with different gifts and roles. All of us are needed—we all have a part to play.

In Titus 1:5-9 and I Timothy 3:1-16, the Biblical injunctions for office of Deacon or Bishop are listed, but Bo again felt that this was Paul's feelings on the matter because he was never married—and not what Christ said. It was Paul's day and his feelings rather than what Christ said. But He did say, "The harvest is plentiful, but the laborers are few," Jesus said. "Pray the Lord of the harvest will raise up more laborers." (Matthew 9:37-38) Amen.

Bo went on to say, "Quotations from Christ overcome all prejudice. To put women down is to deny their intelligence." May the self-righteous, the bigots, the modern-day "Pharisees" who think they know—study the teachings and mannerisms of Our Lord Jesus Christ, who saw no distinction between the races or the sexes. In fact, a woman was the first to see the Risen Christ. A woman was the first to receive the declaration, "I am the Resurrection and the life; he that believeth in Me, though he were dead, yet shall he live." (John 11:25) Jesus wasn't just talking about men!! He was talking about mankind! He saved an unnamed sinful woman in John 4, and then sent her as a missionary to her own village!

This does not mean that women should not adhere to God's divine chain of command nor negate it. Christian women still believe in God's pattern for order in the church and home. Bo was still under her Pastor and her Deacon husband, Luke. She readily admitted that her husband was the leader of her home in an humble and loving way, and her Pastor the leader of her church. She never expected it to be otherwise. In fact, this was another first for the church in Roswell, for a husband and wife to both be Deacons simultaneously! Bo and Luke had eighteen families each to tend and shepherd!! They were the first couple to serve jointly in the state of Georgia, according to an article in the *Christian Index*.

The Good Lord allows us to suffer the consequences of our choices so that we will learn our lessons. His high priestly prayer is John 17, yet to be answered, is that we all become "one." We cannot learn merely by reading or studying. We learn from our experiences, from the lives of others, from our own mistakes, and from the Holy Spirit, our Divine Teacher. We indeed reap what we sow. I have learned much from Bo Buice, my mentor. She has taught me not only by her words, but by her example.

Knowledge and revelation are not static, and God continually helps man increase in knowledge and wisdom, and His Spirit interprets scripture and guides us into all truth. What I've been taught is that the scripture is a progressively unfolding revelation; we understand more as time passes and unfolds. Another idea which I've learned lately which is so profound to think about is that just like learning a foreign language or how to use a computer, God also has a language. His language is powerful—if we learn it, love it, read it, pray it, memorize it, speak it and absorb it into our hearts and lives. His language can change our lives!!

"The refining pot is for silver and the furnace for gold, and a man (or woman) is valued by what others say of him (her)." (Proverbs 27:21) People who do not "know" her shouldn't judge her. They should look at the fruit of her life: teacher for 30 years, inspiring younger people to think and learn; Sunday School teacher for nearly the same length of time, having a class named for her; many, many spiritual children; a wonderful sense of humor; wonderful lifelong friends as well as always making new ones; a constant witness to the love of Christ and the importance of the local church, fairness to all people regardless of race, religion or sex; member of the same church for over 60 years; wife to her only husband for 61 years; mother to Ervin (Jason); and step-grandmother to three grandchildren and six great-grandchildren. Finally, she is a retired Deacon for 10+ years, serving the Lord's people under the supervision of three Pastors. Her fruit remains. I thank God for beautiful people like Bo Buice.

Dogmatic legalism should be put out of our churches. Love covers. This doesn't mean that we throw away the law. Jesus said that He didn't come to do away with the law, but to fulfill it. The law is our "schoolmaster" to bring us to Christ, but once we are His, we need to put on the attributes of love, forgiveness, acceptance, forebearance, excellence (not sinless perfection, for no one was perfect but Christ), and we are to take up our cross and follow Him daily, and love people, not crucify them!! God help us all to be more like Christ is our relationships. Jesus is indeed the answer for the problems in the world today. He is the Way, the Truth and the Life. He is not "a way." He is "the Way." Jesus is "the only begotten Son of God" (John 3:16) who loves us all equally (the world) that He gave His life that we all might experience eternal life—if we will receive Him into our lives as Lord!

This is what Bo Buice did when she was approached on being a Deacon at First Baptist Church Roswell. She asked herself, biblically, could she be one?

Well, if you only read I Timothy 3, you would come to the conclusion that Bo would have been disqualified. But, if you consider all the scriptures on the subject of women in leadership positions, then you would come to a different conclusion, especially if you considered the culture in which Paul lived and ministered. Women were considered second class citizens then. They were treated like "property" and continue to be today in certain parts of the world. Plus the fact that Paul was not married. More than once, in the New Testament, Paul forbade women to talk in church. (I Timothy 2:11; I Corinthians 14:34,35) Well, if we were to take that literally today in our churches, we would have a real problem. The women do as much, if not more of the work of the church as the men. If we look at this passages from Joel 2:28 & 29, which is repeated in Acts 2:17, 18:

> *"And it shall come to pass in the last days, saith God, I will pour out of my Spirit upon all flesh: and your sons and **your daughters** shall prophesy, ... and on my servants and on **my handmaidens** I will pour out in those days of my Spirit; and they shall prophesy."*

(To prophesy means to speak forth truth—not to predict the future necessarily.)

As I am stretched out on my bed with my laptop on my "lap" and as I hear the spring wind blowing the wind chimes on my porch, these thoughts are rushing through my mind: The times they are a changing; the winds of change are blowing in our homes, land, culture, and churches, and we must somehow come to grips with the changes taking place. If there is one thing we all know for certain—change is a part of life, and those who can adapt to change seem to fare better than those who cannot. God told us in His Word that His truth endures to all generations. (Psalm 100:5b) Truth endures, and God never changes (Jesus Christ, the same yesterday, today and forever); so the message—the old, old story doesn't change—but the methods of how to reach people do change with the passing of time. We need to get in on what God is doing today. Solomon lamented in the Old Testament, that "there is nothing new under the sun." But God said, He is doing a new thing! "Behold, I make all things new!" (Revelation 21:5)

His mercies are new every morning!! (Lamentations 3:23)

In conclusion, I read an article in "Enjoying Everyday Life" Magazine by Joyce Meyer Ministries in which author Loren Cunningham was quoted from his book, ***"Why Not Women?"*** in which he states, "Some women are called to be leaders; some are called to be homemakers. Women must have the freedom to obey God and be fulfilled in the gifts He has given them." Actually, Mr. Cunningham, some women are called to be both leaders and homemakers, like myself, for instance. God is always first and my family and home next, but then there is the ministry which I've always tried to do, but have been held back often times because of my sex. And I am definitely not a feminist—let it be known loud and clear, and neither is Bo Buice!!!

Mr. Cunningham went on to say, "Rejoice in whom God has gifted. **My heart's desire is to see the mightiest missionary workforce in history unleashed. As we release women, we'll mobilize the hundreds of thousands of people needed to complete the Great Commission!"**

Bo ended by saying, "God is still creating you and me in His likeness. I feel sympathy for Eve. I, too, am always reaching out to things that look great, wanting to know more than I know now. But in the garden of our lives, He still speaks and guides us—if we are listening."

So how do we reach the "lost" people? We reach them by love, acceptance, prayer, by Christlikeness. He was winsome because he was compassionate, caring, loving and patient. He didn't hit people over the head with the laws of God. He gently told them about a different way of living—a kingdom where the rules are opposite to what they are accustomed to here on earth. In His kingdom, the way up is down, the way to win your life is to lose your life in service to others. The one thing Jesus was hard on was hypocrisy. He "hated" the actions of those who professed to know God, but their attitudes and actions proved that they did not. This "Pharisee" spirit is still in the world today, as those who profess to be in the kingdom often turn away the ones who are in need of the Answer.

In finding the answers to life's complex problems, one must first realize that when God created the world, He did not leave people without instructions. He gave us His written Word to read (The Instruction Manual) and the living Word (Christ) to watch and hear. In studying the Bible, where the Word is proclaimed to be "the Word of God" more than 866 times in its pages, we must never take one scripture out of context in order to prove a point. We must study all related passages to obtain the clear interpretations. We also must consider the culture in which something is written. So we ask the questions: What did this mean then? What does it mean today? What does it mean to me personally?

If you are a woman reading this book, and you have felt "squelched" in being able to use your talents for the edification of Christ's Kingdom, as I have often felt, then we both must ask ourselves, "Am I fulfilling the call that God has for me and if not, why not?" What is your passion? Go forth and finish the work for which God has given you to do. This is exactly what I am doing in writing this book: fulfilling a passion which has lain dormant for a very long time. I'm reaching out by faith and trusting God with the outcome. What is your dream? Like Bo Buice, go for it!

> "What we all need is a simple relationship, not a complicated religion."
>
> —Actor Pat Boone

BO'S DEACON ORDINATION SPEECH

It is difficult for me to express how I feel tonight. I am happy and proud and I am humble and concerned.

I have done much thinking in the last few weeks. I believe that I am a positive thinker, but never in all my plans did I think I would stand here tonight. Some of my thoughts have been regarding what other people think. But early on, my thoughts turned to my parents. Naturally, they had a strong influence on my life. My father was a progressive Baptist minister, a step ahead of his day. My mother was good in all her roles. Since I know that tonight they are in the realm where we'll understand things better, I feel sure they voted for me.

I accepted Christ when I was 10 years old during a revival in Hickory, North Carolina. I believed as a 10-year-old believes. During my teen years, I wondered about things and doubted some. When I went to the University, I became interested in the Baptist Student Union, both at a local and state level. At a BSU retreat, I committed my life to Christ.

At that time, I was considering two important decisions:

I was considering being a BSU Secretary on a college campus and I was considering marrying Luke. I cast lots and the lot fell on Luke. From that day until this, that was my finest decision. On our wedding day, we knelt and asked God to go with us in our marriage, and He has done just that!

I think that on this occasion, I should simply share some of my religious beliefs. I was reared in a Baptist home, but I am a Baptist today by belief and conviction.

1. I do believe in an omnipotent God who manifested Himself in three ways. He is my Creator and your Father and mine. Since He is our Father and is good, He shows no partiality toward His children.
2. I believe that in order to know us, relate to us and save us, He came in Jesus. Jesus lived, died and rose again that you and I may do the same.
3. I believe Christ did not leave us but that He came to us in the Holy Spirit. He is with us tonight.
4. I believe that every believer is a priest. I was a priest before I was a deacon. We have direct access to God.
5. I believe that the tithe is the Lord's. If you want to support goodness and righteousness, there is no fairer way.
6. I believe that God revealed Himself in the scriptures.
You and I have a right to interpret it for ourselves.

The Bible did not fall from the skies during the reign of King James. The scriptures came to us through human minds and hands inspired by God.

In creation God's greatest gift to us was freedom of choice and will. When He inspired the writers, He used them with their human strengths and weaknesses. Each was limited to his ability, talents and personality and to his locality and generation. This in no way limits the Eternal Truth of God's Word found in the scripture. The same God who inspired the writers inspires you and me to study to find the truth. The scripture is a lamp unto my feet and a light unto my path.

7. I believe in the church, the universal church which crosses all denominational boundaries. But I believe firmly in the democracy and autonomy of the Baptist Church. We have always had to fight forces from within and without that would take from us our freedom. I love this church (RFBC). I hope this church will never surrender to any power other than the Man, Christ Jesus.

I am not sure what credentials I bring to the office of deacon. I've been looking for some. I've been trying over a period of time. I was chosen out from among you. There are 60 active who have been chosen. If you lean toward inerrancy, you know that the scripture says, "choose seven." (Acts. 6:3) Sixty is the correct number for our church. The Holy Spirit did not stay in the first century. He is our contemporary. He guides us to meet the needs of this church in this day.

I did not seek the office of deacon. But I firmly believe that God's call and His service is unlimited. I believe that from creation until now, any word that was written or spoken that shows discrimination toward any person is not of God, but of man. God is no respecter of persons.

I love this church. We are all one in Christ Jesus. I thank you for your vote of confidence. I ask for your prayers that our church may be strengthened and may rise to higher ground.

FIRST BAPTIST CHURCH

710 MIMOSA BOULEVARD
ROSWELL, GEORGIA 30075

587-6980

DEACON ORDINATION SERVICE

November 8, 1987

"WE ARE ONE IN THE BOND OF LOVE"

ORDINATION SERVICE

November 8, 1987
7:00 p.m.

Piano Praise	June Nelson
Hymn 202 "Make Me a Channel of Blessing" (Smyth)	
Welcome & Announcements	Rev. Bo Prosser
Quartet "Serve the Lord With Gladness" (McKinney)	
	Luke Buice Jerry Songer
	Bo Prosser Jerry Tyler
Hymn 405 "We Are Called to Be God's People" (Haydn)	
Offertory Prayer	Jim Stewart
Offertory	Selected
Report of Nominating Committee	Marvin Whaley
Report of Deacon Body	Keith Brasher
Report of Ordination Council	Earle Vick
Testimony of Candidates	Murray Griffin
	Rodger Johnson
	Bo Buice
Installation of New Deacons	
Charge to Candidates	Rev. Brantley Seymour
Charge to Church	Dr. Jerry A. Songer
Solo "A Call: A Prayer, A Promise" Jason Buice	
Hymn 298 "Lord, Lay Some Soul Upon My Heart" (McKinney)	
Laying On of Hands All Ordained Deacons & Ministers	
Ordination Prayer	Joe Carl Johnson
Approve G.B.C. Messengers	
Right Hand of Christian Fellowship	

Deacon Ordination Service Bulletin at RFBC in 1987

Article in the Roswell Neighbor about Bo becoming a Deacon, with Emily Dolvin's signature on the article. (Emily is former President Carter's aunt and Bo's neighbor)

Bo & Luke are honored at RFBC for their years of service;
award presented by Steve Baker

"Christian Women, Come Rejoicing"
Bo Whitener Buice

(Hymn sung to the melody of
"Hark, The Voice of Jesus Calling")

Christian women, come rejoicing,
Raise your standard high today.
Christ has called us, lift your voices;
He will guide us all the way.
Bring to Him your gifts, your service.
Claim His goodness, love, and power.
Thank Him, praise Him for His mercy,
For this day, your shining hour!

Lord of all, we seek Your presence,
Honor Jesus Christ, the Son.
On our efforts pour Your blessings
For in Christ we all are one.
Help us heed the Great Commission,
Trust your word, its truths make known.
Make our homes your site of mission,
And our hearts your royal throne.

Christian women, come rejoicing!
The inner court is yours always.
Praise Him, praise Him, lift your voices
For your night has turned to day.
Pray for women of all nations,
For in Christ we all are free.
Savior, make us new creations;
Mold us, make us more like Thee.

Poem Bo wrote about "Christian Women Come Rejoicing"

Some of Bo's Teachings

DEACON TRAINING—10-3-93

The job I have accepted is uncharted. I don't have a map. But a new church year gives us all a new opportunity. We have been elected to a very responsible job. I didn't do as much last year as I wanted to do. But I do know this being a Deacon is more important than being ordained. It is more responsibility than honor.

I believe that each of us want to do a good job. Being good and efficient on any job requires genuine interest and knowhow. Knowhow requires training. Step I in training is to see that you don't know everything. You could use some new ideas. It is not right to accept a job as responsible as our's and sit back and hope for real success in growing a great church.

Some of us have attended the 500 Training Sessions. Some is not enough. Our church really needs a new surge of interest and commitment. The Deacons can make it happen. With effort, we can all be better than we are. We can be swinging. Training is for everybody, and requires effort. Don't ever again come to a meeting expecting to hear nothing and leave to do nothing.

During this year I plan to have a 15 minute training period at each meeting. I hope we will all participate and improve on the basics. Some of these are:

1. Loyalty to church
2. Ministry to people
3. Stewardship of time and money
4. Leadership Responsibility

Scriptures support the things I've said. If we all go, think of the impact it will have on this church and on us.

I have prepared a chart to remind and urge us along through the year.

FAMILY MINISTRY—BO'S TEACHING—10-31-93

At each of our meetings we want to think about some practical ways to actually plan to improve our service as Deacons. It is proper tonight that we place our emphasis on our Family Ministry.

Christian is our calling. Deacon is our classification. Service is our job. Ministry was not our idea. It came from the heart of God. We find encouragement in Luke 10:1—"After this, the Lord appointed seventy others and sent them out two by two ahead of Him to every city and place where He wanted to go." In other words, He needed help. He sent them ahead to introduce Him, not just to every town, but to every family. He explained why: "Because the harvest is great, but the laborers are few." (v.2)

We are not the 12 disciples. Nor are we the 70 called out. We are some of the others whom He has sent out through the centuries. In Roswell First Baptist He wants to go to every family. He will go primarily through you and me.

I don't believe that any group of deacons has ever done a 100% job of ministry. Let's be the first. We will receive helpful suggestions at each meeting on how to minister. We will succeed only if we remember that He has sent us.

GIFT OF SELF—BO'S TEACHING TO RETIRED TEACHERS, CHRISTMAS, 1985

Peter Marshall once said that serious minded people cannot spend Christmas, observe Christmas, but keep Christmas.

Year after year we let Christmas slip away from us for 11 months. Suddenly it's here again! Frantically, we get ready to celebrate by doing many unnecessary things and by worrying about gift giving. To whom? What? How much shall we spend? A large percentage of gifts are not useful, needed, nor appreciated.

In His Eternal Plan, the Great Giver gave us the reason for Christmas giving, but we earthlings depend on a calendar to tell us when to begin.

Celebrations the world over often show little understanding because in our hearts the knowledge of Christ, God's Gift, is so limited. Remembering should cause us to seek more knowledge and use His eternal plan.

Alex Pope in his Essay on Criticism II, wisely urged this search for knowledge. "A little learning is a dangerous thing. Drink deep or taste not the Pierian Spring. There shallow droughts intoxicate the brain and drinking largely sobers us again." Drinking largely in gift giving means that with each gift we must give a portion of ourselves. We need to revise our list, eliminate swapping and duty-giving and concentrate on gifts that carry a part of us. Gifts must be personalized. In each gift is concern of giver for the concern of receiver. Let me illustrate the degree of concern. Suppose that next week I become suddenly ill or have a serious accident. If you know me, and am my friend, how could you respond? When you hear:

1. Feel some concern—then dismiss it.
2. Ask someone about me.
3. Sign your name to a printed card or send a note, which is more personal.
4. Call me—use time, finger and voice.

These are graduated signs of giving and concern. But if you know my needs and really care, what could you do?

5. You would come to me and bring me something of yourself.

What a difference coming concern makes!

Now back to our knowledge of the Eternal Christmas Plan—God, soon after creation, saw the needs of His creatures. He made many efforts to reach them:

1. He raised up judges—they felt some concern, but distance was too great.
2. He appointed Kings—Detached, no interest, impersonal, like the printed cards.
3. He sent Priests—who spoke to God for the people and made sacrifices, like the personal notes.
4. He sent Prophets—They called the people with personal contacts.

All these gifts helped but the deep needs of the people were not met.

Finally God said, "They'll never know me 'til I go." And in the fullness of time He came in the Person of His Son Who dwelt among us and gave Himself for us. Our Teacher and Example—the Greatest of all Gifts—The Gift of Self.

Marco Polo tells the story of how wonderfully and appropriately Christ gives of Himself. The Magi or Wise Men came from a village in Persia seeking the Christ. They were magicians and curious to meet the Great Magician. One was very young, one middle-aged and one very old. When they saw the Christ, they gave Him their gifts. The Young Boy found a young Christ, a learned and lovable friend, who gave him hope and joy and a reason for living. The Middle-age Man found a Christ his own age, a friend, who knew responsibility, hardship and hard work. Christ took hold of his daily load and helped him carry it. The Old Man found a Healer, a Christ who understood and healed his illness and removed his heartache, renewed his strength and gave him peace and the promise of eternal life. Each gave a costly gift, but found in Christ the answer to all his needs, which was a priceless gift.

So this Christmas, we can at least wish to drink largely from the well of this eternal plan, change our thoughts and methods, knowing full well that "the gift without the giver is bare." He who gives of himself feeds three: himself, his hungering neighbor and me.

Life's most worthwhile relationships are formed not by impersonal obligations met, but by gifts of time, courtesy, kindness, thoughtfulness and love. These gifts are wrapped with Divine love and are delivered by you and me. The return address on each of these selfless gifts is: The Christ. "When you have done it unto the least of these, you have done it unto Me," Christ declared.

Eternal God, we thank You for Your unspeakable Gift and the joy we experience at this Christmas Season. Grant us the wisdom and the will to see Christ this Christmas. Lift us this day from our self-centered plane to your level of giving and living, we pray. In Christ, Amen.

Some of Bo's Students Reunite to Celebrate her 87th Birthday at the Founder's Club in Roswell

In attendance: (l-r)—Winifred Smith, Linda S. Miles, Delores M. Lashley, Margo Coleman, Elaine Coker, Carolyn Banister, Diane Dorris, Saundra Brumbeloe, Shyra Pruitt, Margaret Ovbey

Linda Mansell Martin, Bo Buice (87) & Barbara Garrett

Bo's Students Share What She Taught

B o was coming out of a Deacon Meeting at church where a former student of her's, Brian Ivey, commented that Bo was his school teacher at one time in the fifth grade at Roswell Elementary. Bo asked him, "Brian, what did I teach you?" He rapidly replied:

"To thine own self be true and it must follow as the night the day . . . . Thou canst not then be false to any man." (Shakespeare) *Hamlet* I, 3

Back then, Bo could teach the scripture, the very best literature, and she grieves that the Ten Commandments, prayer and Bible reading have been stricken from the public schools.

One day in her classroom, a little child taught her. Many of the other children had brought her gifts for Christmas, but this little child didn't have a gift to give her. He timidly approached her desk, and presented her with a little pencil drawing—all that he had to give, which she kept to remind her that "it is more blessed to give than to receive." He actually gave himself to her that day, to show his love for her the only way he knew how. She kept this little drawing as a reminder that even the poor have something to share.

One of the Church Secretaries at Roswell First Baptist, wrote Bo about one of her teachings in Sunday School dated January 2, 1994:

Dear Bo:
Just wanted to tell you how much I appreciate you! You will probably never know how much your class means to me. You are an

inspiration to me. My journal is 'peppered' with gems from you and I added to it today your interpretation of Jesus' response to Satan when tempted to turn the stones to bread.

"I'm not that hungry yet."

I love that! Add that to the choir's challenge ("May all who come behind us find us faithful") and it's a wonderful challenge for the new year. Be faithful—even in your "hunger." Whatever the temptation, be faithful.

God bless you in '94.

Ira Humphries . . .

And another one:

Dear Mrs. Buice,

I think about you many times when I am teaching at the elementary school. We have a real secret garden. I will always remember you reading "*The Secret Garden*" to us after lunch as we listened to the FUMC chimes. Thanks for the memory.

Love, Carol Hawkins Reddish

Byron J. Foster, formerly of Huntsville, Alabama, after moving to Roswell with his young wife and year-old daughter, joined the Bo Buice Sunday School Class, and remained there for the next 17 years, saying, "It's obvious that I loved her class because she was very intelligent, well-read, and stayed current on world events." Even now that they have moved away, they still stay in contact with Bo. Byron wrote:

I will never forget the time she asked me to teach the class. I had never taught a Sunday school class before, and I was very reluctant to accept. She kept insisting, saying, 'I know that you can do it . . . .' so I had no choice. I accepted. Here I was teaching a couples' class composed of professional men and women and at the back of the room sat Bo Buice. Her comment to me after the lesson was, "I knew that you could do it."

Another young man whom Bo has had great influence is Dan Curry. Dan and his wife, Margie, originally from Ohio, visited Roswell First Baptist, and sat in front of Bo. He politely moved over so she could see, and after the service, Bo asked if they were members, to which he responded, "This is our first Sunday to visit."

Well, sweet Bo proceeded to give them the full spill about how wonderful the church was and how they would be so happy there if they decided to join. She eventually introduced them to everyone, and Dan and Margie felt very welcome. Dan said that they joined her class and she "learned" me how to be a Christian, both by her teaching and her example. They both love to tease each other. Dan "adopted" Bo just as so many before and after him have. They became fast friends. Like me, Dan's mom had died, and he felt drawn to her.

Dan has helped Bo immensely at her house with odd jobs and such. Additionally, he helps Pastor Ron with many visitations and other helpful tasks at church. I told him that I know his spiritual gift is "helping," to which he humbly admitted to be true, saying, "I love helping other people, because I care about them." Because he works from his home, he is able to be flexible in his scheduling.

He and Bo have a little game they play, because she loves Snickers candy bars, and he "sneaks" them to her. One day in church, sitting beside her, Dan noticed one lying inside her pocketbook, and he teased her about it, and they both almost made a scene laughing about her "hidden" snack. Dan and Margie gave Bo a stuffed monkey, named "Snickers."

They had to rush Bo to the hospital one day, when she was in a lot of pain. In the emergency room, when the doctor finally came in to check Bo for abdominal pain, Dan noticed that he didn't even feel her stomach and followed him outside the room to quiz him on that decision. The doctor admitted he didn't understand her problem and came back in. She was immediately rushed to surgery, where they performed surgery on her colon which had perforated the stomach wall. Dan was probably instrumental in helping to save her life, to which Bo will always be grateful. (Dan, could it have been caused by all those Snickers?)

Dan is eternally thankful to Bo and First Baptist Church for getting him on the right track. He admitted that before coming there, he was on the fast track chasing the "Almighty Dollar," instead of the Almighty. He is so grateful to have peace, joy and love in his life to replace the stress, emptiness and void he once had. He admitted his only regret is that he didn't find them sooner.

Dan never had the privilege of meeting Luke, but he did meet Jason, and was impressed by his beautiful voice. I know Jason must have been thankful for Dan, in times when he could not be there with his mom, knowing people like Dan were there when she needed someone. We're all thankful for people, who help others, like Dan Curry.

—

Scott Law, Bo's hairdresser from 1985 to 2006, said that he recalls the first time Bo called the shop where he was working—"Catherine's" and Bo asked for an appointment with Catherine. Scott informed her that Catherine was busy and he offered, "What about me?" Bo asked if he could use rollers, which he answered affirmatively—and which he is still using to this day on her hair. He says she still tells him how to roll and color her hair after all this time, but that is the teacher in action. Scott owns his own shop, Voila, in lower Roswell, only minutes from Bo's house. Scott is also quite an artist and another wonderful "helper."

Thomas Tolbert approached Bo one day in Scott's Salon, and reminded Bo of the time she sent him to the Principal's office. Bo chided him, "Well, if I sent you, you must have needed to go!!" Of course, neither of them remember why.

On one visit, Scott asked Bo," Why can't we all serve one God? There is only one God isn't there?" Bo agreed with him.

Actually Scott was right in that there is only one God—but what people have a hard time accepting is the Trinity, the three in one God, the Father, Son and Holy Spirit which the Bible clearly teaches. All three manifestations are called "God" in the Bible. It's like I'm a mother, a wife, a sister and a grandmother but I'm still one person, wearing a lot of hats.

Jesus said there was one way, shocking everyone who heard Him when he declared, "I am the way, the truth and the life. No one comes to the Father but by Me." (John 14:6) The wisest man who ever lived next to Jesus was Solomon who wrote, "There is a way *which seems right* to a man, but this way is the way of death (spiritual and physical)." (Proverbs 14:12) Some folks want to come to God their own way instead of the way God required.

The way is narrow; it is difficult, but the way leads to life—abundant life. The broad way is the popular way which the masses prefer because it is easier and more acceptable. But it is the wrong way; it is the way to destruction, according to Matthew 7:13-14. "Few" will find the way which leads to life and home, Jesus said.

Yes, there is only one God. One of His name's is "I Am." He is whatever you need. His name is not "I will be" or "I was." He is one God with many names to describe His characteristics. The problem comes when people don't accept what He teaches and requires. So through the centuries, they've made for themselves "a god" more to their liking, one that is more acceptable and comfortable. This "god" becomes an idol in the truest sense of the word—a god of one's own making. The One True God who made the world and everyone and everything in it is too difficult to accept by the masses, too narrow, too demanding, too hard to understand apart from relationship and study. So many come up with all sorts of ways to make Him more acceptable. He no longer is God, the One and Only, but "a god" of one's own design, and in truth, a false god.

All this can be illustrated by a situation in which my husband and I were involved. We owned and raised a beautiful little tabby, tri-colored kitten we named "Madeline." She was very beautiful, playful, loving and carefree, could climb trees in a flash and was friendly to everyone, even all our eight grandchildren could pet her, and she would lie down and let them. She would lie beside me as I studied and come in each night to be "petted" by my husband. She lacked for nothing and was truly loved and protected.

But she had one fault—she wouldn't stop wandering. She got it from her grandmother; wandering was in her genes. She was always looking for "a better way," or "another way," "a different way" home. She wanted something else but what she had been given. She was always on the prowl for something more.

One night she wandered away—never to return. We were devastated. She was our precious possession, whom we'd invested with a lot of love, attention and blessing. But she was gone never to be seen or heard from again. Destroyed. Forever.

What happened to Madeline? Several days afterwards, we saw a large coyote, stalking at the edge of our property, seeking "who he may devour." We've seen him several times since then, and my husband discovered their den—more than one living in a den on a cliff overlooking a small creek at the back of my neighbor's property. We know that the coyote "tricked" our pretty kitty, due to her always unfulfilled curiosity. She just wouldn't obey us and stay home. She didn't understand her enemy. She believed she was free to do and go anywhere she wanted, and we would protect her. Wrong. We couldn't. She mistakenly thought we'd always protect her and save her, which, in fact was only partly true. Anytime I saw her crossing our street, I'd go and get her and bring her home, lovingly scolding her. But she wouldn't stop her bad habit. We'd always love her no matter what she did, but we couldn't always keep her from harms' way. That was her choice to roam, to leave the safety of our home and go looking for more. She chose her fate, and it was a terrible one. The only way we could possibly have saved her from the coyote was to become a cat ourselves, and teach her about the dangers of straying.

So it is with God. He loves us always. Protection is under His loving wings. But He gives us the choice to go our own way, a way that may not be the best way or the safe way. In having that choice to go and do as we please, we can really stray off the straight and narrow path and get into real trouble because our Enemy, Satan, is always on the prowl, like a roaring lion, seeking whom he may devour. (I Peter 5:8) Just like the coyote, he is lurking, waiting, watching to seek us out when we are oblivious to trouble, just like our little carefree kitten. The Enemy comes to steal, kill and destroy. (John 10:10) That is his mission; that is what he does endlessly, tirelessly, increasingly. You'd better watch out for him, especially you young ones. Don't be deceived by his cunning ways.

So yes, there is One God. But He is the One and Only God of the scriptures, who has chosen to reveal Himself therein to those who will seek and look for Him, He will be found by them. "Ask and it shall be given unto you, seek and you shall find. Knock and the door will be open unto you." (Matthew 7:7)

Bo's Means of Transportation

Dan Curry & Bo

top: Elwyn & Jewel Gaissert
bottom: Bo, laughing, and Luke, Norma Strawn

How Others Relate to Bo

By this time in our story, you have probably gleaned much from what you've read about our heroine. She does relate well to people.

Recently at a Sunday School Retreat led by Rev. Bo Prosser, a friend and former Associate Pastor at RFBC, during one of his sessions, we determined that Bo Buice's personality temperament is that of a "Puppy." She is an extrovert, optimistic, always friendly, loves people, has lots of friends, loves to tell stories, is the life of the party and needs a lot of praise! Wow, fits her perfectly. As all personality types have strengths, they also have weaknesses. Her weaknesses are that she might tend to jump to conclusions, get by in life on her charm and personality, may tend to exaggerate, to dwell on trivia, is often disorganized and forgetful. This, too, describes Bo to a tee. She saved everything but it was in disarray, and I had to try and put all the many pieces of the puzzle of her story together. One sentence in the handout Bo Prosser gave us jumped out at me about "puppies," "Quit being so darned charming and help out every now and then!"

All people have strengths, and we all have weaknesses. I have chosen to major on Bo's strengths in this book, because her strengths by far outweigh her weaknesses. Following are some words which others have said to and about Bo.

> Dear Bo:
>
> There are very few people that I really admire, but you are one person that I do. I've always admired your great faith and your service to our Lord. I'm not sure that you realize how many people you have helped in finding their faith. I have always admired your sense of humor and your kindness, your love and devotion to Luke and Jason. I have a wonderful mother, but if things had been different, I'd liked to have had you as my Mother.
>
> Love, Sylvia P.

Dear Mrs. Buice:

"I wanted to say 'Thank you' for the lessons you taught me many years ago. I share the Christmas Story with my children each year (and it's one I don't have to read). I will always remember who taught it to me."

Love,
Susan Smith Branan

From Mrs. Dee Lashley:

I wanted to share a story about Mrs. Buice that I always think of when I think of her. She is a very wise woman. She is, to me, the personification of a genteel Southern woman . . . . one who thinks before she speaks:

One thing I remember most about her was something she said to our Sunday School Class many years ago when my children were small. She told a story about her son, Ervin, returning home after being away for a while when he was a young adult. When he came in, they were shocked to find that he had grown a thin mustache. Apparently, this change in his only son was too much for Mr. Buice to bear, and began to chastize him for this new look and offered him money to shave it off.

After some conversation with her husband, Mrs. Buice admonished him by saying that it was totally inappropriate for him to allow an inch of hair to come between him and his son, that he was a good young man and a mustache was not going to change what was in his heart.

I related this statement to my own sons later when it became fashionable, or a fad, for boys to allow their hair to grow long. I told them that as long as they kept their hair clean and brushed, that I would allow them to let their hair grow. They behaved well, had good hearts, and made their mom proud of them.

Along those same lines, I received an e-mail from Ervin's first wife, Judi, who had this to report:

I remember that Bo was rightly proud of her talented and handsome son and always wanted to show him off whenever we went "home" to Roswell. She would manage to arrange for Jason to sing in church on Sunday (which he disliked). It was my role to smooth the way and talk him into doing it to please his mother . . . . of course, when everything was over, Jason enjoyed the solos as much as she did, and all the accolades he received, and he was glad that she asked him.

One year, the arrangements nearly fell apart when she and Luke were horrified to see that he had grown a mustache and had longer hair (this was the style in the 70's, after all). When her pleas (evidently, she was as upset as Luke was!) to shave prior to the Sunday service fell on hostile ears, she gave up and Jason sang in his "new" look. Rev. Brantley Seymour saved the day when he thanked Jason from the pulpit for his wonderful solo and noted that he liked his new mustache!

The following is from Randall B. Brannon, former Principal of Mountain Park Elementary School, from an article which he wrote in the *Roswell Neighbor Newspaper*:

Do you remember that special teacher who brought out the best in you? I am sure you can tell the name of that teacher and the class he or she taught. Aren't you amazed at the impact that teacher had on you and still has? Perhaps there were several. I can readily think of two. Mrs. Buice, my fifth grade teacher at Roswell Elementary School, and now my neighbor, who encourages me to this day, and Mrs. Harry, my history teacher at Roswell High. I cannot tell you why they stand out. Perhaps it is because they believed in me.

Perhaps it is because they had high expectations. Whatever the reason, I am especially grateful at this time of the year (Thanksgiving), for their continuing presence in my life.

Take the time to thank your child's teacher. I know that I am grateful for the dedication of today's teachers. While you are at it, take the time to write a former teacher of yours. You cannot imagine the feeling you give to a teacher with a simple written thank you. Make a difference in that teacher's life. It is the least that you can do.

Yes, Randy, these were two of my favorite teachers as well. What I remember most about them is that they were compassionate and enthusiastic.

Here's a rather lengthy but very interesting letter to me on behalf of Bo from her long-time student, now living in Maryland, David Bowen (formerly of Crabapple) who even named his ranch, "The Bo Buice Ranch!"

Dear Linda:

At the age of twelve, in the year of 1952 A.D., I became a student of Mrs. Buice. I'm sure that I looked like every other boy she'd ever seen. However, I had some 'bad baggage' with my entering her class. My Grandmother Bush had died recently and I suppose I acted out some hostility as a result. We were very close, my Grandmother and me. Of course, at that age a little boy doesn't understand about death.

As the year dragged out, I became more and more noisy and disrespectful to all the people around me, especially Mrs. Buice.

Well, at some point she got fed up with my behavior, quite understandably, and sent me down to Mr. Jasper Dolvin, our Principal. This immediately got my attention since Mr. Dolvin was about six feet, four inches tall and weighed way over two hundred pounds! In my young eyes, he was very threatening.

When Mr. Dolvin invited me into his office, he was very cordial as he inquired of my reason for being there. I immediately informed him that Mrs. Buice was 'picking' on me and that she probably 'hated' my even being in her class.

Mr. Dolvin replied that he understood my situation and invited me to go with him down to the post office which in those days was located across from the downtown Roswell Square.

As we proceeded down Mimosa Boulevard in his almost new 1949 Chevrolet, Mr. Dolvin never said a word and looked straight ahead. We finally got to the post office, and he instructed me to remain in the car. By this time, I was really getting concerned because I thought he would have whipped me with that paddle he had in his desk drawer when I first entered his office.

What was he going to do with me? Take me to the Police Station? I reasoned I hadn't done anything that bad!

After what seemed like a very long time, he returned to the car with the school mail. He made a left turn at the Roswell Store, then a right turn at Jake Coleman's (Linda's Uncle's) filling station, and headed back to school.

When we pulled back to the original parking place, I was somewhat relieved. However, I anticipated now the "hurt" coming from the paddle!

We walked still silently back to Mr. Dolvin's office. As we approached the doorway, he looked down at me and said, "David, I know that you are going to do well the rest of this year in Mrs. Buice's class and also you will go on to the eight grade and high school. Now, I want you to go back to Mrs. Buice's class and tell her that you won't be giving her anymore problems in the future."

In my daze, I replied, "Yes Sir, Mr. Dolvin, I'll do that right now."

When I got back to class, I signaled to her through the little window in the door to come out into the hall. I heard her tell the other students she'd be right back. I immediately apologized and told her what Mr. Dolvin had said of his expectations of my future development.

She said that she totally agreed and that everything was going to be alright!

Linda, the reason for this little story is because Mrs. Buice and Mr. Dolvin helped to give me direction and what I wanted to achieve in life. Certainly, at the time, I couldn't have been aware of that. But the spirit of accomplishment, I think, dwells in all children. Well, anyway, I went on to graduate high school at Roswell, finished college and got married out on the west coast and raised a very good family (in my opinion) I attribute my direction and hopefully good decision-making to people like Mrs. Bo Buice and Mr. Jasper Dolvin.

Mrs. Buice and I still are friends to this day, and I truly love her as a loving and wonderful giving woman, a woman who has devoted a lot of time trying to improve the human condition.

Hopefully, any positive thing that I can do will be the "ripple effect" of the kindness and direction that I have received from people like Bo Buice.

David was a faithful member of Bo's Sunday School Class for many years, and still stays in touch with Bo by phone and mail.

May 31, 2006
Dear Bo:

You are one of the most special ladies I know. Thank you so much for letting me be your friend.

For several years after my wife and I had come to Roswell, long before I joined the staff of First Baptist Church, I kept hearing these legendary reports about one Mrs. Bo Buice. I kept thinking that all that they were saying about you could not possibly be true about one person; surely, the comments must be a number of legendary stories about several people, simply rolled together and attributed to a single individual. I soon came to realize that, no, it is true; Mrs. Buice is all that they said, and more!

You really are!

One of my most treasured memories is when you and your son, Jason, moved across the Sanctuary through the pews one Sunday morning to tell me that you were hoping to be on the Associate Pastor Search Committee when it was selected, and how Jason took my hand, shook it firmly, and said that he was praying and hoping that I would be presented to the congregation as the candidate for the position. I did not realize that anyone really was aware of my interest in the position, and I certainly did not expect that anyone would be so verbally affirming of my candidacy. I rejoiced greatly when I heard that you were on the committee, and I cannot begin to express how grateful I was that you and Jason had affirmed and encouraged and blessed me with your words and support. What a blessing it was to hear a few weeks later that FBC-Roswell was extending a call to me become the Associate Pastor!

I am absolutely delighted that you are involved in the preparation of this biography. When I think of the great women of the Bible, the Deborahs, the Hannahs, the Marys, the Esthers, the Dorcas, the Priscillas, and many, many other special women whose stories fill the pages of Holy Writ, I rank you right there at the top of the list with them. Your story and pilgrimage are an inspiration and encouragement to all us who know you. And, much more that, they are a blessing to so many others who know and have heard about you.

Your life has touched and blessed mine beyond measure. You continue to be a special friend and blessing to me. May God richly bless and keep you always, and may He shower you with His love and favor from above.

I love you, dearest friend!

Robert C. Vickers,
Associate Pastor, FBC-Roswell, Georgia

We moved to Roswell in 1971 and became members of First Baptist Church. Bo and Luke became immediate friends and a spiritual influence on our family. When Bo became the first female deacon in our church, she was our family deacon. Our son, Bob, was in China as a missionary journeyman at the time. She served, not only locally, but stayed in touch with him half way around the globe. Bo, you're a treasure. The longer we know you, the more we love you and appreciate your friendship.

Sam & Dora Freeman

P.S. Please reserve a book for us.

Soon after Lee and I joined RFBC in 1977 we learned that Luke and Bo Buice were stalwart pillars in that body of believers. They immediately embraced and welcomed us into their lives and circle of friends.

Luke shared with us that there was only girl in all the world like Bo and that he was blessed to have found, wooed and win her beautiful heart. We too have recognized the sterling qualities of Bo's character and book in the glow of her gracious heart as we are priviledged to share in a treasured relationship that has so enriched our lives . . . as the poet wrote "Some people come into our lives and quickly go, some stay awhile and leave footprints on or hearts and we are never the same" Grateful friends, Lee and Helen Brown

July 31, 2006
Dear Bo,

How precious you are to this church and to me! Thank you so much for speaking at the J-Term class. You gave everyone an insight to how women have function at First Baptist over the years. I can't wait for the book to come out and tell all the history you have seen and made.

Thank you from the bottom of my heart for taking your time and putting your experiences down for us. If it would be possible I would love a copy of the notes you had on Sunday morning for the records.

Love you muchly,
Jan (Moore)

From Dr. Ralph and Eula Langley (former Interium Pastor at RFBC):

"I'd rather see a sermon than hear one any day," perfectly describes Bo Buice. I witnessed her go through some of the hardest adversity possible and handled it beautifully, with a Christlike attitude. She is a masterful Sunday School Teacher."

From Rosemary and Glenn Berry of Ellijay, Georgia:

Our family moved to Roswell and joined FBC in the summer of 1986. Glenn and I were taken to a couples' class taught by Bo Buice. The Buice name was familiar as Luke's older brother had been my Grandmother's pastor in Lincolnton, Georgia, many years earlier.

Never had I studied under a teacher who brought the scriptures to life as Bo. She seemed to take me to places where Jesus had walked and then applied those same scriptures to everyday life experiences. All through my Bible I had written some of her comments in the margins and still refer to them today.

Dear Mrs. "Bo",

You're a collection of all of your years,
your stories, your glories,
your troubles, and tears.
Tales of a lifetime live in your eyes.

You are ninety years wise.

It's Your 90th

Love,
Lara Newton
Mary Claire Manuele
We think of you often
and keep you in our prayers

It is such a joy for me to join with your family & all your host of friends to thank you for your love. I wish you a very special & happy day.
In His love,
Charles "Chuck" Hellen

Charlene & Kineen

4/30/5

Dear Bo,   April 28, 2005
Happy Birthday to you, dear lady! and I hope, pray, and wish for you to have many, many more! You are very precious to Carl Ann and me, and we love you very much. Thanks for being such a dear friend. May God richly bless and keep you.
With much love,
Bob

Dear Bo,
Happy 90th Birthday!
Thank you for being my special teacher and my caring friend!
You have enriched my life.
I love you!
Susan
(and Jeff, too)

Happy Mother's Day
and a Belated
    Happy Birthday
because you've been a
Spiritual Mother to me
and I love you!

    Linda M.

You and your family have meant so much to Roswell First Baptist. Thank you for all that you have done and continue to do.
If I can ever do anything for you, please do not hesitate to call.
    Sincerely,
    Sally White

Happy Birthday dear Bo!!

Thank you for loving us into the Bo Buice Sunday School Class.
    You are an inspiration to us
    and we love you.

        JoAnne + Paul

"...He that dwelleth in love dwelleth in God..." 1 JOHN 4:16

"All the days ordained for me were written in your book before one of them came to be."
Psalm 139:16 (NIV)

Remembering you with much love...
    Nancy and Jim Hyams

Elizabeth Batey
Jewell Dickey
Sarah McC____

Bo,
You have blessed our lives so very much. We thank God for you. Have a super day!
    Love,
    Betty and Bob Swanson

Bo-

You are so very special to me and so many others. Thank you for all your encouragement! Have a very special day!

Jan Moore

To Sweet, Sweet Bo,
a servant for the Lord!
You are always a supporter of W.M.U. & one an inspiration to all of us at RFBC.

With much love,
Sheila Edenfield

Dear Bo,

Happy Birthday to a Living "Saint"! You are such a courageous, shining witness for the Lord in good times and in bad; happy and sad. We love you so very much. We treasure your love and friendship!

Love, Ron & Cheryl Bradley

Be full of love for others, following the example of Christ...
Ephesians 5:2

Helen Jones
Ruth Hall
Alicia Miller

Your and Lord Wishes to a very dear and special person

Peggy Walker

← Bo's PASTOR
MINISTER OF MUSIC →

We are so glad you were born!
We are so glad you came to get us!
We are so glad you paved the way for the ordination of women
We are so glad you are our friend

We Love You!
Tyler and Maryanne

You have meant a lot to Stan & I. You have shown us to love, study, pray and serve. Thank you for your example.
Happy 90th Birthday!

Patsy & Stan Shuford

Thank you for being such a great lady and sharing yourself with others. your life of service is a model to me.
Love, Carolyn S.

You truly have always been an "angel of an Aunt" by, most of all, living the Christian life as an example for us to strive to follow. You have also been an "angel of an Aunt" when you and Uncle Luke have been there for us when we needed you most. Thank you. We *love* you and wish for you many more *happy* birthdays to follow.
Dorothy and A.G.

that the world is an infinitely better place because you're in it... because you're you!

Dorcas McDonald
Sheila Edenfield
Ti Woodruff

to a wonderful friend.
This card must have been written with you in mind. It represents you perfectly.
Love,
Opal Wright

Dear Bo,
You deserve a very special birthday card but I've none to make or write this one. I do hope this 90 th one (published, isn't it) brings special joy to you in ways you never dreamed of.
Gods must love you, the years speak them my friend as these years.

xxxx

You are a very Special Lady and Loved by all who knows you! May God Bless and Keep you is my prayer!
Love,
Liz Halloway

You are very special to us and we thank God for you
Love
Addie Mae + Glenn

Lo, have a great 90th — you don't look like it.
Betty + J.C.

Mrs. Buice,
We love you so and we appreciate all the years you taught us in Sunday School - you were the best teacher we ever had - You were very special to us.
Love
Jane + Jerry Bishop

Dear Mrs. Buice, April 3, 1994
We want to thank you for being such a wonderful teacher and friend.
Our love,
Rosie + Glenn

Dear Miss Lo,
I can't come to your party but I want you to know how much I love you and appreciate your leadership and teaching. You have meant so much to our church and community and we don't tell you enough how special you are. You have been in my thoughts and prayers.

Love Always,
Vicki Neal

You are so very special to me and so many other people!
My love,
Joy

"There is surely a future hope for you, and your hope will not be cut off." PROVERBS 23:18 NIV

Dear Mrs. Buice,

I can't believe it has been almost 30 years since I became one of your students in Sunday School! You made a tremendous impact on the lives of us young mothers, stressing to us the importance of a religious education for our children as well as for ourselves. You helped us to understand the Scriptures and relate them to our lives and you knew how difficult it was for young families to grow, emotionally and spiritually, without good religious instruction. I appreciate your dedication to our class and to the Church. You mean so much to so many. I hope you had a very happy birthday and will have a happy and healthy future.

Deloris (McGahee) Lashley

Proud mother of Kim, Mark and Sean McGahee.
Proud grandmother of Brian and Stephanie Taylor.

04-10-02

Dear Bo,
 What a wonderful role model you have been to us.
   Blessings on you!
     Love,
       Karen & Marvin Whaley

Mrs. Buice,
 You have been a teacher, an inspiration, and a caring friend for so many people. We are especially thankful for you & have meant to us.
  Love,
   Saundra & T.D.

Bo, congratulations on this milestone! You are an inspiration to so many. Your friendship means a lot to me.

God bless you!

Love, Betty Gibbons

11-20-05

Dear Mrs Buice —

I always do.

I think of you often and remember your kindness and gentleness in leading me + others in prayer + bible study. Your mission hasn't changed in all these years. Your are a true reflection of Jesus. Love Winifred

Mrs Buice,
The Bible says God knows what we need before we even ask Him and I believe it. It's true how every need you presented would come to the front. The first time I worked with Sunday School, by your quiet ways how many hearts are touched by everything you do. You'd know the gentleness and love that is always felt by you.

You are a fragrant blessing with God's bouquet of that's why it pushed you on this journey. God loves and every need is done for you.

Martha

Over the years my husband (J.W.) and I loved and respected you as a wonderful friend and Sunday School teacher. You are truly a mother and mentor to so many of us!!

The world would surely be a much better place to live; if everyone had more friends like you in their corner of the world. You are truly a blessing to me each day! Love and prayers
Liz Alloway

Happy Birthday
Love and all good wishes to the best auntie anyone ever had. Every thought of you brightens my day and makes me think you made me.
Clarice

Notes from Friends, Students and Sister

Card From Elnora Seymour   October 4, 2003

Bo,

The special service Sunday in honor of you and Joy was a worthy and well deserved tribute to you both. I hope you know both,

Bo, what you've long since know — your friendship has meant to me and to Bradley, you and Luke were there at the very beginning of our ministry in Roswell, a time when we needed all the help we could get. We had so much to learn and so much to experience, but what it is, I can look back and see — looking together, experiencing God, and feeling God's Spirit guide through all this time of His Word. He is to be loved!

"God is able to make all grace abound to you, so that in all things at all times, having all that you need, you will abound in every good work."
II CORINTHIANS 9:8 NIV

Bo,

May you see your accomplishment as something you can be very proud of, and may you also see it as others see the Lord has blessed your life.

You have blessed my life and I know many, many other people through your teaching in the church and the school. I love and thank God and thank Him for you!

Elnora
(Seymour)

"The Sunset of Our Lives" by Bo & Linda

EVENING

A Celebration of Life

Jason Byce

June 17, 1944-February 13, 2005

Ervin (Jason Byce) Buice's Celebration of Life Program
at Roswell First Baptist Church, Feb. 15, 2005

The Departures

Deaths are part of life on earth. Our lives are a "mist that is here for a little while, and then is gone." (James 4:14) We all have a short time to make a difference in the world, to let our light shine, to find our calling and to be a blessing as Bo has been to so many. As she looks back over her life, she has had many heart breaks, but the blessings far exceed the sorrows. She says that heaven seems so much sweeter the closer she gets to the end of her life and especially since she has so many loved ones "on the other side." "It will be worth it all when we see Jesus."

We have a choice when life sends us tragedy to give up, get on drugs, drink ourselves to oblivion and go to bed, or to trust our Savior, Jesus Christ, to give us the courage to keep on living and serving others. "For a righteous man may fall seven times and rise again," the Proverbs 24:16 teach us. This is what Bo Buice has done through the ups and downs of her life. There are many happy days and many sad ones as we travel the road of life. A close, personal relationship with Jesus Christ is what makes the difference as to how we handle the sorrows and sufferings which come our way, for He Himself was "a man of sorrows, acquainted with grief," and He understands and enables us to keep on keeping on when the sorrows come. He also gives us the courage to keep smiling and to have His joy as our strength. From her earthly father, Bo learned to keep laughing and living "above the circumstances" of life. But her Heavenly Father keeps her joyful, living and giving still today, having outlived most of her relatives. Her church family has become more precious to her in these waning years of her life.—

Reverend Horace Cleveland (Cleve) Whitener passed away on June 19, 1956, at age 70, with an aortic aneurism. He made a lasting impression for good on the lives of his three children and two grandchildren and all his "spiritual" children. Ervin adored his grandfather, calling him "Pops." Bo has a little book with some of her father's sermons written in his own handwriting. I've chosen this one to include here:

WHAT IS THE CHRISTIAN RELIGION?

"Except a man be born again, he cannot see the kingdom of God."
John 3:3

I. It is personal
    It is about a Person (Jesus Christ)
    It did not come by education, or any "ism"
        It is personal—we cannot share it by proxy
    It is about our relationship with Him

II. It is an experience
    Correction for sin
    Repentance of sin
    Faith in Him
    Redemption of our bodies

III. It transforms
    It is available to all
    God's promises are true
    It is not about performance but about
        transformation

Bo's mother, Lela, died suddenly on November 16, 1950, when Bo was 35 years old. Bo's father remarried Alpha Buice, a single woman, who was indirectly related to Luke and had never been married. They were only married for three years. Bo still misses her parents to this very day.

Born December 13, 1912, Henrietta Clarice, Bo's older sister, whom Bo labeled "Cat" when she was small, was more a "Kitten" than a "Cat." Cat attended Bessie Tift College and transferred her senior year to the University of Georgia where Bo was a freshman. Clarice got her degree in Education and taught in Dalton several years before she became a secretary at First Baptist Atlanta to Dr. James Middleton and later to Dr. Louie Newton of Druid Hills Baptist, also known as "Mr. Baptist." She later served on the Baptist Home Mission Board until she retired. She lived in Buckhead her working years. She and Bo were always good friends. Bo has a card which she cherishes that Clarice sent to her in which she wrote, "Love to the best sister anyone ever had. Every thought of you brightens my day and makes me love you more."

Clarice never married, but she had a good life and lived with that half bullet in her brain which the doctors rediscovered at the end of her life when she was in the hospital following a stroke. Clarice spent several years in a nursing home, at which time Bo decided to bring her to her home where she lived and died within a few months.

Bo's friend and attendant, Robbie Wineland, was caretaker to Cat the last nine months of her life while she lived with Bo. Robbie was introduced to her husband, Mike, through Bo at RFBC, and they "courted" on Bo's sun porch. Robbie wore one of Bo's party dresses for her wedding, which Bo had saved since she was a young woman!

Bo and Cat shared many things, including their love for the Lord and for music, with Clarice playing the violin and Bo the piano. Bo says, "I miss her so, like she was when she was well. After she had that stoke, I was so sad." Clarice Whitener died May 23, 2004 at the age of 91.

Horace, Bo's brother, also attended and graduated from the University of Georgia. He worked for Ford Motor Company and married Mary Brannon (Whittingham) from Atlanta. Mary was very intelligent and cute. She and Bo shared several classes together at the University of Georgia. Mary and Horace had one son, Cleve, named for his grandfather. Cleve graduated from Westminister High School, but was diagnosed as manic-depressive, dying in his 40's. Mary went to bed with arthritis after his diagnoses, had a rather sad life, dying in her 60's prior to her son's passing. Dying from lung cancer in his 40's, Horace and Bo were very good friends as long as he lived and shared many wonderful times together. He had a beautiful voice and sang in the choir at First Baptist Atlanta. MaryEm remembers Clarice and Horace from her time at First Baptist Atlanta, and what wonderful people they both were, very involved in the church.

Bo also had a famous aunt, Catherine Evans Whitener (1880-1964), her Daddy's brother, Will's wife, from Dalton. She is credited with becoming the "mother" of the carpet industry in Dalton, Georgia, the mountain town known as the carpet capital of the world. This worldwide industry began with the production of chenille, which Catherine is credited with starting, who was quoted as saying, "I see my work as a calling, but I used it to make a living." As a teen, already an accomplished seamstress, she saw an unknown coverlet with a weave foreign to her, bought some muslin, heavy thread and a large needle and proceeded to replicate the stitch. She pulled the thread through the fabric, clipping each stitch with the scissors, leaving little tufts of thread, and "wa-la" chenille, the famous embroidery design was born. Later, the carpet industry incorporated the idea into their carpet manufacturing!! Most of the carpet industry is 90% tufted today, a process that grew out of the chenille bedspread industry. About 80% of the U.S. carpet market is supplied by mills located within a 65-mile radius of Dalton.

On our trip to Virginia, we met one of Bo's only living relatives, a cousin, Susan Whitener Gardner, daughter of Tom Whitener, Cleve Whitener's youngest brother. Susan, now living in Arlington, Virginia, is the widow of Jeoff Gardner, who died 7 years ago from cancer and is buried at Arlington Cemetery in Washington, D. C. Susan and Jeoff had one daughter, Cindy, who is married to Ryan and they have one daughter, Marlee. Bo, Nelle, and I lunched with Susan at a wonderful French restaurant on our trip to Washington, and enjoyed hearing her share her life with us. Susan's Dad, Tom, sounded like an interesting man who wore many hats before his death: Professor at Stetson University and Director of Admissions, worked for the CIA, worked in Atlanta at Emory Medical School, and finally for TWA. Susan is quite the hostess, and loves entertaining folks. She and Bo enjoyed being together that day so much, since there are so few "Whitener's" left. Susan remembers young Ervin, standing and singing at the foot of the stairs in a little white suit. She talked about her father and his siblings: Ed, Cleve, Willie, Aunt Cathy (the chenille lady), who are all gone now.

Luke passed away on October 11, 2001 following a series of illnesses. Bo affectionately reminisces as she talks to his picture in her bedroom. "We were truly one," she proclaims. "Sixty-one years with someone is a real record today. I miss him so."

Jason (Ervin) was first diagnosed with non-Hodgkins lymphoma in fall of 2003. It started with a severe backache, nausea, chills and fever.

In August, Jason and MaryEm sang the popular song, *"You Raise Me Up"* at the opening faculty meeting at Smitha Middle School. As he left the stage, knowing that none of the teachers were ready to be back at school, Jason raised a waving hand and quipped, "I'm leaving now but, Ya'll have fun now, ya' hear!" Getting his laugh he left the stage and drove to Atlanta for his three month check-up with his Oncologist. Later that afternoon while attending the opening game of Hannah's fast-pitch softball season MaryEm's cell phone rang. It was Jason with the results of his blood tests—results that this time were far more serious than before! She felt frozen in time as she heard his voice say the words, "Baby, it's Multiple Myeloma ... I'm having chemo even as we speak". He responded well and went into remission with the lymphoma.

For at least two weeks prior to January of 2004, he had just not been himself. MaryEm knew he had been battling cancer for a couple of years, but mentally, she had noticed a change. He had been taking a very high-powered pain killer, and she attributed the change to that until she was informed that his electrolytes were compromised severely, which caused his alertness to wane. If that weren't enough, he was experiencing unbearable pain in his body and feet, caused by nerve damage as a result of the chemo.

From Christmas 2004 until January 21, 2005, Jason underwent tests at Northside Hospital where they discovered a fracture on his leg bone. He was in the hospital for three weeks. While he was at Northside, I was in the rotation to take Bo to the hospital to visit Ervin for one of the last times, on February 10th, as I recall. He was taken to ICU that night after his heart stopped. Bo brought him fresh squeezed orange juice to drink, which he did, saying, "Um. m.m good." Bo just insisted that I come in and see him, even though I was apprehensive. I loved him, but wanted to remember him healthy, laughing and well, not sick and in pain. He seemed to recognize me, and had that big, warm smile on his face, even in the last stages of his illness. As I looked at the 89-year-old mother comforting and "petting" her 60-year-old son, I wondered why it couldn't have been the other way around. But then I remembered that God is in control and knows best because He sees the big picture. He holds the keys to life and death.

February 12th, he was transported to Piedmont Hospital in Atlanta. MaryEm stayed with him until about four o'clock in the morning, sitting in the dark and "coldness," wondering, praying, hoping. A wonderful female doctor from emergency took charge of him, and gave MaryEm the opportunity to go to the waiting room to sleep awhile.

At 8:00 the next morning, Sunday February 13, a nurse called her and said she might want to come back in the room now. She went over to the bed, as he looked up to her with that same loving, "no-sick-day-expression," and that winning smile and said to her, "I love you," and that's the last thing he ever said to her. She replied, "I love you, too, and you're doing so much better," which she thought he was, to which he responded, "I am?"

With everything going well, Allyson and MaryEm went down to the Snack Bar at about noon for a quick bite of lunch. The Nurse said, "Take your time." They didn't and were back in the room within thirty minutes. Immediately upon entering Jason's room MaryEm detected tension among the nurses and, when she looked at the monitors she knew the reason why! Jason's blood pressure had fallen drastically!

The Inhalation Therapist was manually pumping oxygen into his lungs and, saying repeatedly, "Mr. Byce . . . Breathe! Mr. Byce . . . Breathe!" "Breathe, Mr. Byce!" These are MaryEm's words:

> "As I stood there, numb with grief over what my deepest fears were telling me, my heart cried out to God, "**please, help Jason**"! My prayers of the past two years flooded my memory . . . "Lord, you know my

heart and what **I** want to happen . . . **I beg** you to heal my beloved husband"! I remembered how at the same time I kept hearing His voice saying to me, "Be still and, **know** that I am God" . . . and, how I would obediently close with, "Lord, may Thy will, not mine, be done in Jason's life . . . Amen

Snapping back to the moment, I realized that God **was** answering my prayers! I felt God's presence in that room and, He **was** helping Jason! God, in His infinite love, was relieving "our" loved one of all of his physical, mental and emotional suffering and calling him home to be with Him. There would be no more pain from the ravages of cancer for him, no more denials following auditions and, no longer having to settle for jobs that didn't allow him to use his God given talents of singing and acting!"

Bo was upheld by Dr. Bradley as they stood on one side of Jason's bed and MaryEm and Allyson on the other as they watched as he peacefully passed into eternity later that day.

They were all brokenhearted but in time were comforted by the promise of heaven for believers. As MaryEm said, "We will be reunited someday and will stroll hand in hand through Paradise, harmonizing eternally. We must 'Keep a song in our hearts.'"

MaryEm hurts when she hears women complaining about their husbands, especially now when she has lost two of them! She says, "You are so fortunate to have your spouse. Every minute should be cherished, the good and the bad." She learned with her first husband's death, that it doesn't matter that he doesn't pick up his socks. That is a small thing. We must learn to appreciate each other, and "accentuate the positive, and eliminate the negative," as the song says, while we have each other.

She was 36 when her first husband died; he was seven years older than her. He was on the faculty of West Georgia College her senior year, and they dated. She had to be removed from the cheerleading squad because she was not allowed to date the coach of the team for which she was cheering!! She was asked to make a choice, and she choose John.

Looking back, MaryEm says John and Ervin (Jason) were two totally different people. The first date she had with John, she thought to herself that he is the kind of person that I'd want to marry. He was the "salt of the earth," never said a cuss word, alcohol nor cigarettes never touched his lips. He was such an inspiration to the boys he coached, and just 'a good old mountain Tennessee boy, just precious.' They were married for 15 years, and had three beautiful, wonderful children. The children were at the center of their lives, and they probably didn't make enough time for each other.

THE DEPARTURES

Right before he died, on a Friday night, when MaryEm had done a sacred concert at Olive Springs Baptist Church in Marietta, and John came. That night when they got home, and he and MaryEm were standing in the kitchen, he put his arms around her and hugged her, saying, "Honey, one of these times, when I'm listening to you sing, I'm just going to stand up and start shouting, 'Hallelujah.'" That night they talked about how they just had to start making more time for just the two of them. The next morning, he left to go down to their 210 acre property in Carrrollton, to cut the grass and never came home. She called the Sheriff that night. They found his body up on the roof of the house where he had gone to fix the t.v. antennae and had a massive heart attack. He was forty-three years old.

After John died, MaryEm was so intent that her children not suffer and that they would still have a good life, and devastated though she was, it kept her strong and determined. She said that they kept him alive in their thoughts, and talks. To this day, they still have stories and memories that they share about their father and her first husband. When they tried to understand why this man in the prime of his life, who was giving so much to others as a good father, coach and leader would be taken at such a young age, she came up with, "maybe she and the children could be a blessing to others to show them what the love of God can do even in the times of great sorrow." She and her children started singing at churches, banquets and different places as living testimonies to the strength of God in weak, hurting vessels.

MaryEm feels so blessed to have had two such wonderful men, so different in many ways, but both so special in their own way. She feels now, with Jason's departure, to be so fortunate to have loved and been loved twice, and wants others to see Jesus in her, and to let others know what peace and strength He can impart when the time comes when we need Him most.

=============

Ervin's (Jason's) memorial service was the largest group of people that had ever been in attendance at Roswell First Baptist Church. Rev. Larry Adams, who had also married Jason and MaryEm, had a large part in the "celebration" of his life that day—February 15, 2005.

As MaryEm and her family drove to Roswell for the service, she gave this speech, "Okay, kids, there will be no tears today. I want a smile on everybody's face. Today is Pops' day, and we want to make him proud of us. She was driving his car at the time, and as she lowered the sun visor, in the church driveway, his sunglasses fell out, and she said, "We all lost it." Therefore, they cried ahead of time!

Ben Cybul, MaryEm and Jason's grandson, gave one of the several eulogies on behalf of his grandfather, "Pops." Here are his words:

FOR "POPS"
By, your loving grandson, "Begs"
February 13, 2005

As we sit here today, to Almighty God we pray...
To escort our loved one, into his land of eternal sun.

Jason Byce always was and always will be,
One of the greatest men you will ever see.
An amazing life that he lived the best that anyone could,
We think back now to where that great man once stood.

His spirit is instilled in all that knew him,
We know that he would have given support, life and limb.
Just to save what we hold dear,
He valued all others' wishes over what he held near.

Now, I ask you to do the same,
To remember how he stayed true, even in his fame.
To live once more in the days when he was here,
To laugh and live and to know you have nothing to fear.
As long as his great essence filled the room,
No eyes could weep or heart feel gloom.

And now I leave you with what would be one of his last requests,
To remember him for all your times together, goods, bads, and bests.
But finally, as we all must part,
He is calling back that he loves us all, and to always...

"KEEP A SONG IN YOUR HEART"

Ben's Poem About Pops which He read at
Jason's (Ervin's) Memorial Service

There were many of Jason's students in attendance at the memorial service, wiping their eyes and recalling the influence he'd also had in their young lives and promising careers. Jason's love came through to the young people under his influence because of his enthusiasm and zest for living, just as his mother's and grandfather's before him.

A friend of MaryEm's daughter, Allyson, said after the service that she was so "down" because "my husband and I don't have that kind of love." The hurt of it was probably magnified because of the time of the year, Valentines. Husbands and wives must teach each other and "break in" each other, as my husband says. Loving does not come naturally. It is the highest Christian virtue, and it is more a decision than a feeling most of the time in marriage because life is hard, but God is love. He teaches us how to love each other, if we are teachable. We have to "plant" what we want. When we "plant" love, we harvest love. When we plant hatred, sarcasm, selfishness and pride, we harvest the same unwanted attitudes. Of course, it does make a difference if you marry the "right" person, MaryEm said. God can make us all into the "right" people if we will let Him.

MaryEm went out of her way to make sure that the dept of feeling and love that Jason had for life and for people would come through. She said he told her one time, "I know you love me, because when I walk in the room or come home, I see it on your face." Another friend told her, "I used to love to look at Jason when you were talking, and he was watching you, because he took so much pleasure in you." Their relationship was very, very special. Oh that we all could learn from their examples and that of Bo and Luke's, of the importance of loving people, and especially our spouses while we still have them in our lives.

Scott Law, Bo's beautician for 16 years, came to her home and "did" her hair for the funeral. It's a good thing that he did, because she received so many people that day, that the line was the longest I'd ever seen at one funeral. It literally looked to be a mile long. She greeted everyone with such love and motherly affection, as if we were all her children!

The Memorial Service was quite a production, beginning with a recording of Jason singing from the Cherub Choir, to eulogies from several family members, with a film of his commercial, "Please pass the jelly!" There were CD's given away of some Christmas songs he had recorded. There were letters read, Eddie Sullivan read the "Red Clay and Honeysuckle Poem" which Jason wrote and talked about his friend and "brother." There was an entire row of his friends from the Class of '62 from Roswell High School sitting together. And there was music!!

God holds the keys to life and death, and only He knows the days we are given. "All the days planned for me were written in Your book before I was one day old." (Ps. 139:16 NCV)

As I re-read the Christmas, 2004 newsletter that Jason always sent out to his friends and family, one sentence grabbed my attention (see the end of this chapter.) This was written just weeks prior to his death. The Lord must have needed a new Choir Director for the heavenly hosts, who praise Him continually. In January of 2006, I dreamed I was in a large church and Jason was directing the choir. When he saw me, he came over and hugged me, as he always did when our paths crossed on earth. I sensed he was saying to me, "I know what you are doing in writing my mother's story, and I thank you."

MaryEm had just retired from teaching music and chorus for 29 years, and her last school concert as of December 14, 2004, and celebrating the Christmas season was capped off by a surprise video presentation on her life and career by her colleagues. Many of her former students were there to say how much their lives had been touched by her influence both personally and in the classroom.

Jason had been teaching voice and drama at Kennesaw State University. He commented in his Christmas newsletter that his singing had gotten better due to his teaching. That reminds me of a quote by Robert Frost, "I teach in order to learn." In addition, Jason drove charter motor coaches for American Coach Lines. He said that it allowed him to "clear away the cobwebs." My husband, Alan, and I had seen him in the last year driving a small bus at Big Canoe for their Tour of Homes. In fact, we were passengers on his bus, and I sat behind him and we chatted and renewed old friendships. I think this was in the summer of 2003. That was the last time I saw him prior to that day in the hospital in February of 2005.

MaryEm ended by saying that she had loved and been married to two men. She was married a total of 30 years, 15 years to each one, and that she had loved them both. She says she feels so sorry for those who've never loved deeply. Our Pastor, Dr. Ron Brandley, counseled her saying, "It doesn't matter the length, but the depth of loving, not the quantity of time invested but that the time you had together was quality." Plenty of people have 60 or 70 years of quantity time, but the quality was not what it could have been due to many factors—most of which involve selfish pride.

In MaryEm's words concerning Jason's dog, Captain: "Jason got Captain, his little dog, when he was performing at the Burt Reynolds Dinner Theater. He went to the pet store with his co-star, Linda Michelle, and he said that Captain just sort of "wuffed his name". He named him Captain because that was the character he was playing in the show, ***Little Mary Sunshine.*** " Captain was his ONLY family off and on for 16 years (other that Bo and Luke). I mean the only family that was WITH him. Captain had acted strange for a while . . . just not himself. Then one morning he just collapsed on the kitchen floor . . . couldn't stand up. Jason took him to RB Garrett in Roswell. He stayed there for a few days . . . . the diagnosis was cancer of the liver. Jason came by to my school room in hysterics on an April Wednesday of 1998 (I remember because we were supposed to leave for All-State that afternoon and Hannah had the Chicken Pox that year) and said that Captain had to be put to sleep and I must go with him. So, I called the school secretary and told her that we had a family emergency and went with him. When we arrived, due to the blood he had been given Captain was frisky and looked great! So, Jason immediately thought he's better and maybe we won't have to do anything. But, RB told him he wasn't getting any better. So, RB prepped Capt. and left us alone with him for goodbyes. It was heart wrenching! Jason wanted me to hold Captain while he gave him the injection so that is what we did. We then took Captain over to Bo's and buried him right at the edge of the driveway in the backyard. Then we went to Savannah . . . not a delightful trip."

Jason sent out a beautiful poem about Captain and his death that he had written and they received many sympathy cards.

> "When the sun goes below the horizon, he is not set; the heavens glow for a full hour after his departure. And when a great and good man sets, the sky of this world is luminous long after he is out of sight. Such a man cannot die out of this world. When he goes, he leaves behind him much of himself. Being dead he speaks." (or sings!)
>
> O. Beecher
> (*Streams in the Desert*, June 1)

> "When we get all high and mighty and think that we truly are the masters of our destiny, it only takes one little reminder, one little tap on the shoulder from the One who made us to bring things back into focus."
>
> —Jason Byce
> Newsletter, 12/04

> "Why shouldn't we go through heartbreaks? Through these doorways God is opening up ways of fellowship with His Son. Most of us fall and collapse at the first grip of pain; we sit down on the threshold of God's purpose and die away of self-pity, and all so-called Christian sympathy will aid us to our deathbed. But God will not. He comes with the grip of the pierced hand of His Son, and says, 'Enter into fellowship with Me; arise and shine! If through a broken heart God can bring His purposes to pass in the world, then thank Him for breaking your heart."
>
> —Oswald Chambers,
> My Utmost for His Highest, Nov. 1

RED CLAY AND HONEYSUCKLE
By, Jason Byce

REFRAIN:
All the "Cheer" and "Tide" in Georgia can't remove that deep red stain,
And that sweet smell on a summer night tends to draw you back again.
Now, I've been thru hell and I've smelled Chanel, but all that can't compare
To red clay on my shoes...and sweet Honeysuckle in the air.

^^^

I grew up on a river; Chattahoochee is its name.
And the lessons that it taught me to this day still remain.
I've traveled far and I've seen it all; but I never will forget
The red clay on my shoes...and the honeysuckle when it's wet.

My Daddy owned a hardware store; my Mamma taught grammar school.
Tho' they tried real hard, I've made mistakes; but they didn't raise a fool!
For the good town-folk instilled in me what can't be taught in school:
Fairplay, hard work and honesty, and understanding the Golden Rule.

My roots are deep and sturdy; bad storms they've withstood.
"And when I weigh the "up's" and "down's"...I've had it pretty good!
But when I'm down and need a boost, I recall a sweeter day,
When honeysuckle bloomed in the month of June, and my shoes were in red clay.

I've tracked that red clay up and down, abroad and coast to coast.
It's hard to put a label on the place I've liked the most.
But when I'm through and the show is done, I look down and start to grin;
'Cause I know those tracks walkin' on that stage will lead me home again.

Not long ago I made the move...I came back to that dear place.
I found the girl I'd known since 3, her same sweet way and pretty face.
We tied the knot and joined, for good, our lives and families dear;
And now it's finally come full-round: love, happiness and career.

MaryEm, my wife, my love...the one who brings it all together...
Can change the clouds and rainy days into fair and sunny weather.
Allyson, John and Jayson...oh, and Ben and Hannah...what a crew!
I never knew life could be so fulfilling...so good and wonderfully new!

And my faithful dog, Captain, who's traveled with me many a mile...
He always knows just when I need a warm lick that gives me a smile.
He's slower, doesn't hear so well; the "not now's" are now "well, okay's";
I'm glad he can share his final days with people who love his doggy ways.

That town has changed (I knew it would), but it hasn't lost its charm.
The people there are still the same: true, friendly, strong and warm.
And that river still flows as calm and deep to the Gulf of Mexico
As it did back then, when I was ten, just a few short years ago.

The Poem Eddie read at Ervin's Memorial Service about Their Long Friendship

June 28, 1956

GEORGIA BAPTISTS — 4—The Christian Index

DEATH:

H. C. Whitener

Horace Cleveland Whitener, former secretary of evangelism for the Georgia Baptist Convention, died last week in a hospital at Rome where he had been ill for almost a year. He was 70.

Dr. Whitener retired Jan. 1, 1955, after serving for 10 years in the evangelism office which had reported each year a continuing increase in baptisms. The Georgia Baptist churches reported 33,369 baptisms for his last year, the record high at that time.

In an interview at the time of his retirement, Dr. Whitener said:

"My motive all along has been to try and honor the Lord in all my preaching and in every work I did. I look back now and see the Lord's blessings."

PASTOR: Dr. Whitener was pastor of the First church at Buford when elected to the evangelism office. He had served there for 20 years and had led in the erection of the sanctuary and educational building which still is in use.

He had served several terms on the Executive Committee of the Convention and also on the Georgia Baptist Hospital Commission. Before going to Buford, he was pastor at Morganton, N. C., and Hickory, N. C.

One of ten children born to farm parents in Whitfield County, Dr. Whitener's formal education ended at a one-room school. He left home to find work in a store in Dalton and later was a salesman for organs and pianos in North Georgia and East Tennessee. He was 27 when he experienced the call to preach but previously had given a good bit of his time to leading music in evangelistic services.

DOCTORATE: Mercer University honored Dr. Whitener in 1952 with the Doctor of Divinity degree.

Funeral services were held in Atlanta last Thursday and burial was in the family plot at Dalton. George C. Gibson and R. T. Russell, former associates in the Department of Evangelism, officiated.

Survivors include Mrs. Whitener, three children, Miss Clarice Whitener and H. C. Whitener, Jr., of Atlanta, and Mrs. E. L. Buice of Roswell. The first Mrs. Whitener died in 1950.

H. C. WHITENER

Dr. Horace Cleveland Whitener's Life (1886-1956)
as Described in the Christian Index

Article about Bo's Aunt Katherine Whitener,
Mother of the Dalton Carpet Industry

THE DEPARTURES

Ben wrote this piece about "Blackbird" for his Advanced Music Class About His Grandfather

"Blackbird" is a song originally written by the Beatles, a good song in its on right. But an arrangement of it done by the King's Singers is absolutely amazing. The voices are so crisp and pure, it makes the song so light and airy, adding another layer to an already great song. The arrangement done by the King's Singers is especially important to me because of the sentimental value it holds. It was originally introduced to me along with the full works of the King's Singers by my role model.

The man who is responsible in a big way for my love for music and my aim towards working for the rest of my life with music. This man, my grandfather, Jason Byce, influenced me so much as far as tastes in music is concerned.

The first time I saw and heard this song performed was a wake up call. I finally realized what I had actually known in the back of my mind for so long. It showed me that all of these songs I had heard sung so beautifully on tapes and cd's for all those years didn't do justice what someone could do with a voice and a desire to express emotion with it.

The lyrics have a deep hold in my life in many ways. I am waiting and just existing until I can do what I really want to do, even if only a moment . . . . Also the lyrics seem to be words stated by my grandfather. He (Jason) had been in the same situation at my age when he was reflecting on how to do what he loved—sing and act. In this way and many others this song reminds me of much happier times and easier days, when I could listen to music and hear it, but not let it sink in. This is the first song that I let seep in and I did it because of my grandfather and it is for that reason the track, if you will, for my life."

Song: Blackbird Lyrics

Blackbird singing in the dead of night
Take these broken wings and learn to fly
All your life
You were only waiting for this moment to arise

Blackbird singing in the dead of night
Take these sunken eyes and learn to see
All you life
You were only waiting for this moment to be free

Blackbird fly, blackbird fly
Into the light of the dark black night
Blackbird fly, blackbird fly
Into the light of the dark black night
You were only waiting for this moment to arise
You were only waiting for this moment to arise

Captain, Jason's dog—1993

Madeline, our cat (2005-2006)

OBITUARIES

MARIETTA

Jason Byce, 60, actor known for 'jelly' role

By HOLLY CRENSHAW
hcrenshaw@ajc.com

Jason Byce shared the stage with opera greats Richard Tucker and Robert Merrill. He sang and acted in Broadway musicals with Shirley Jones and Lainie Kazan. He had roles on "All My Children" and other TV soap operas and on series such as "In the Heat of the Night."

But to many people, his biggest claim to fame is a 21-year-old commercial for Polaner All Fruit, where he delivers a line that has inspired imitations from countless would-be comedians at breakfast tables across the nation.

In a down-home drawl that shocks his haughty dining companions, he asks, "Would ya please pass the jelly?"

The commercial still airs on television.

Mr. Byce, 60, of Marietta died Sunday of multiple myeloma at Piedmont Hospital. The body was cremated. The memorial service is 3 p.m. today at Roswell First Baptist Church. Roswell Funeral Home is in charge of arrangements.

"We would be out at a restaurant and somebody would look at him and lean over and whisper to the person next to them," said his stepdaughter, Allyson Cybul of Marietta. "So he would just say, 'Would ya please . . . ?' in that voice, and they would laugh hysterically. People were always asking him to do that."

Armed with a master's degree in voice and opera performance from the New England Conservatory of Music, the Roswell native — born Ervin Luther Buice — amassed a repertoire of 25 operatic roles that he performed throughout the United States and Europe. During a busy stage career in New York, he sang and danced his way through many musicals.

Family photo
Jason Byce plays a difficult opera singer in Theatre in the Square's 1991 "Lend Me a Tenor."

"He didn't wear his credentials on his sleeve and seldom made mention of them, but he was a very influential person in theater and movies," said his friend Larry Adams of Cumming.

"We all want to know someone who knows someone who knows someone, and Jason was always my claim to fame because he knew everybody — all the main players in Hollywood and all the prominent actors and producers and members of the Screen Actors Guild," he said. "But he was the most faithful and loyal friend, and he never forgot you, no matter what."

In 1991, Mr. Byce returned to Atlanta, continued to act at Marietta's Theatre in the Square and other local venues, and started coaching theater students.

"When Jason walked in the room, it was like somebody turned on a spotlight because he was just so fun to be around," said his wife and childhood sweetheart, MaryEm Byce. "He had every reason in the world to have an ego, but he didn't."

Survivors include his mother, Lela "Bo" Buice of Roswell; two stepsons, John Burton West of Augusta and Jayson Charles West of Greensboro, N.C.; and five grandchildren.

Jason's Obituary in the Atlanta Journal and Constitution

Luke & Bo Growing Old

Growing Old

B o just celebrated her 91st birthday on April 28, 2006 at a gathering of some of her friends from church and former students. These are some of her thoughts on aging:

> "Growing old is a true gift from God. Christ died for us; we die to our sin; and then we die physically and return to Him—the reality of death. Recently, I have been thinking differently about death because they (my loved ones) are there.
>
> In my younger years, I never dreamed that I would live to be 90 plus. The years have been filled with kindness and thoughtful acts by all my friends and family.
>
> I look forward to each new day with anticipation. Someone will come and bring food. Someone will call. The mail brings sweet notes and cards. Someone invites me to breakfast, lunch or dinner.
>
> Losing my family has been extremely difficult. I need Luke, Jason and Cat. But their going has made me look forward to joining them in heaven . . . ."

Grow old along with me . . . the best is yet to be . . . . the last of life for which the first was made. Our times are in His hands who said, 'The whole I planned—youth shows but half. Trust God, see all, nor be afraid.'"

—Robert Browning

In youth we learn, in old age, we understand.

(unknown)

"Old age is like climbing a mountain. You climb from ledge to ledge. The higher you get, the more tired and breathless you become, but your view becomes much more extensive."

—Ingmar Bergman

On a recent trip to Ireland, I came across a saying there that has made an impression on me, and which goes along with Bo's famous poem:

> 20 years a growing
> 20 years a shining
> 20 years a stooping
> 20 years a dying . . . .

The Bible says, "The days of our years are threescore years and ten; and if by reason of strength, they be fourscore years, yet is their strength labor and sorrow; for it is soon cut off and we fly away . . . ."

Psalm 90:10 KJV

Moses wrote in Psalm 90, "Lord, Thou hast been our dwelling place in all generations . . . . for a thousand years in Thy sight are but as yesterday when it is past and as a watch in the night . . . . they are like grass which groweth up. In the morning it flourisheth and groweth up; in the evening it is cut down, and withereth . . . . so teach us to number our days that we may apply our hearts unto wisdom."

Bo's friend and secretary at RFBC, Ira Humphries, wrote her a note: "Your life is a wonderful witness to the peace that the 'hope of heaven' brings. You're a remarkable lady, and I am blessed to know you."

"Don't stop laughing because you grow old; grow old because you stop laughing. Don't let aging get you down. It's too hard to get back up."—Unknown

Josephine Miller of Roswell wrote, "It seems that the Heavenly Father looked down upon a precious baby girl and endowed her with special gifts which would make her an exemplary woman. She was graced with beauty, charm, good character, family and friends, good health, honor, intelligence, integrity, wit and wisdom. With love for all people and a servant's spirit, she is a Christian example to all who know her. To know her is to love her. Her name is Bo Buice."

In January, after the occasion of their 50th Wedding Anniversary in December, Luke wrote Bo a card in his beautiful handwriting, containing the following message:

How God has worked in our lives to allow us to celebrate 50 years together:

1. *He made us so that we are compatible.*
2. *He brought us together.*
3. *He strengthened our union by giving us Erwin*
4. *He kept us safe and reunited us after World War II*
5. *He has given us faith that sustained us and kept us in times of distress, physical and otherwise.*
6. *He has led us to a commitment of our lives to Him and the Church*
7. *He has blessed us materially, with work, health, our home, our families, many wonderful friends, all of whom have given richness and meaning to our lives.*
8. *He has sustained us with Faith, Hope and Love,—for 50 wonderful years! 1-4-90*

Love, Luke

Happiness keeps You Sweet, Trials keep You Strong, Sorrows keep You Human, Failures keep You Humble, Success keeps You Glowing, But Only God keeps You Going!

"It is a strange thing that, while all would live long, none would be old," Benjamin Franklin observed.

"Trust no one, not even the finest saint who ever walked this earth; ignore him (or her) if he (or she) hinders your sight of Jesus Christ."
—Oswald Chambers
"My Utmost for His Highest" 3/29

"How far you go in life," George Washington Carver taught, "depends o your being tender with young, compassionate with the aged, sympathetic with the striving and tolerant of the weak and strong. Because someday in life, you will have been all of these."

"Learn from those who've traveled farther down the highway of life. None of us will live long enough to learn it all on our own."—Linda M. Martin

Winifred Smith, a member of the Bo Buice Sunday School Class at RFBC told Bo that she was "much loved" because she has "loved much." Amen.

Another elderly African American woman, Martha Washington, who worked for Bo for seven years when she was a teen, went on to finish school and college at Bo's encouragement, and has thanked Bo ever since for the difference this made in her life.

On June 6, 2006, Bo and I visited Myrt Knuckes (age 85) at the Roswell Nursing Home and made pictures. Then we visited Essie McKenzie's room. Essie who is also African American and is also "way up there" in age, and has just one son who lives away. But her grandson calls her regularly and checks on her. As Bo and I were leaving after our visit, she followed us outside on her little "scooter." She had just said, "Now this is why church family is so important." She is very lonely many days, but because she's a member of our church, she isn't forgotten!! As she "tootled" after us, she got off the sidewalk and her little car toppled over, throwing her to the ground, and thankfully on the grass. She came through unscathed, but almost made me have a heart attack!! I said, "I know why that happened. You were just having a really bad day until we came, and you just needed some excitement!" These little old people still have so much to offer if those on the fast track will just stop long enough to listen to them!! I told Bo that there is something worse than losing one's family, and that is having a family who forgets you when you're old! She agreed.

Prayer: "May God give us grace to live according to His true, holy will, for in this life together, there is only emptiness compared to the spiritual joy that God grants to those who put their entire faith and trust in Him. O God, who is in heaven, O Holy Creator, grant us to taste Thy kingly sweetness in our hearts for, however long the day, the night is sure to come. The day of our death is in store for us too. May God grant us help to meet it." Amen.

—Micheal O'Guiheen
in "A Pity Youth Does Not Last"

BO'S MEDICAL RECORD—4/28/15

Tonsillectomy—1927 (Emory Clinic)

Appendectomy—1937 (Frank Wells)

Nasal Polyps—1944-49 (Dr. Calhoun McDougal)

1954—moved to Bulloch Ave.

Hysterectomy—1955—Dr. S. Glibson

Thyroidectomy—1955—Dr. Letton

Lapendectomy—rt. ear—1955—Lester Brown

(Menopause)

Foot (planter's wart)—1992—Dr. Clark

Hip (left) replacement—1996—Dr. Tom Price, Surgeon

Hernia—1998—Dr. John Harvey, Surgeon

Lower Intestine (10 inches) Oct.—'03—Dr. Jameson

Dan & Margie Curry came and took her to the hospital N.Fulton and they operated.

Eye Surgery—'05—cataracts—Dr. Heit

Jim & Margaret Ovbey took her to the N. Fulton Hospital for these two surgeries

High Blood Pressure Problems—Hospitalized N. Fulton Jan. '06 Dr. Eubanks, Primary Physician

Low Blood Pressure Problems—Internal Bleeding—June, '06 Anemia

Bo wanted this included so people can see that we can keep going, despite hardships and health issues.

Bo also has her teeth at 91 thanks to her Dentist, Dr. Barry Vlass of Roswell.

MATURITY
BO'S TEACHING—RETIRED TEACHERS
MARCH 15, 1990

When I retired I gave most of my teaching aids to other teachers. I reluctantly removed a poster from the wall on which was printed one word: T H I N K. You and I spent many years encouraging children to think. In our period of reflection today, I want to remind you and me that in retirement we must continue to think.

Getting older (maturing) isn't all bad! It's a great part of life. I like the viewpoint of Robert Browning: "Grow old along with me, the best is yet to be. The last of life for which the first was made. Our times are in His hands, Who said, 'The whole I planned. Youth shows but half. Trust God sees all, nor be afraid.'"

Luke and I have been blessed in retirement. We are together and well. We are very busy. Retirement has given us choice in the use of our time.

As a group, we are all blessed in having experienced both youth and age. In many ways, smarter than ever—only if we still think—purposely think. We all want life to be full. So we should think carefully about what we do. Phillip Bailey observed, "He lives most who thinks most." As we mature, it's easier to do things that require no thinking: go to the same places, eat the same foods; read the same part of the newspaper. We've lived long enough to have been exposed to new ideas and to develop many interests. But we are best able to know what's good by doing things that force us to think. Maturity tends to develop a mindset. We aren't always correct in what we think. We need to avoid critical and negative posture and always reciting past events. Live and think in the present.

In reflecting, I decided that some old suggestions can be helpful:

Reading widely gives me pleasure, helps me to see more than one side of timely issues and forces me to think.
Good music, not organized noise, affords good thoughts, which encourages participation.
Thoughtful people make us more thoughtful.
Exercise is the secret of health.

In other words, we need to do things that stimulate us to think, and sometimes change our minds. We have seen much of our world change drastically because people began to think. Henry van Dyke said that the best things come to us as a result of thinking:

"It is only by thinking about great and good things, that we come to love them. It is only by loving them that we long for them. It is only by longing for them that we are impelled to seek after them. And it is by seeking after them that they become ours."

We all have the ability and experience to nourish great thoughts. The Holy Scripture advises us to think of whatever is highest and best because whatsoever we think, so we are.

Paul, writing to the Christians at Rome (and Roswell) said, (and I translate), "I beg you to present your bodies a living sacrifice." This is the only way you can worship and serve Him. "Be not conformed (shaped or fastened) to this world, but be transformed (shaped against, formed anew, changed!" How? "By renewing your mind." Change your thinking!! Make it new. Then Paul says, "You will be able to know and find the perfect will of God."

This fall I want us to polish some old ideas that are good and use them. But the ideas that tell you to do the minimum required, leave them behind. With desire, vision, and new thinking, we can find transformation. In the greatest of all literature, the story is told of two men who find themselves in the Promised Land. The older man's name was Abraham and the younger was Lot. Abraham let Lot choose where he would locate. He selfishly chose the fertile plain near the Jordan. But God spoke to Abraham, "Lift up your eyes and look from the place where you are. North, east, south, west and all that you can see, will I give to you and to your children." So today, look from the place where you are. Your vision determines your claim. There are really five points to a compass: north, east, south, west and the place where you are standing!

There are always higher mountains to climb and unlimited spaces to explore. Civilization marches ever forward on the wheels of education. Today is important. Those in charge must constantly take stock, because more children are coming!!

God has altered my lifestyle—I am so rich—rich in my family, my education, my teaching years, my friends, my responsibilities that have continued into retirement. I have found happiness in all of these. A special blessing is my Sunday School Class. I hope that my choices have helped me make high commitments. "One thing I know with the passing years, one knack I possess—I'm standing for more and falling for less."

I have not always chosen wisely nor have I always kept my commitments but God has kept His to me and I give all praise for my rich happiness and all praise and honor to the "Touch of the Master's Hand" on my life.

James R. Lowell said, "Not failure, but low aim is crime." Let us all look backward and profit, look at today and evaluate, but look forward and work. Tomorrow will be the future."

Eternal God: We thank You for life, for educational opportunities and for new experiences. Help us to direct our thoughts to that which is best and highest. Amen.

Bo and Luke – 7-1-01

Luke   Bo   Cat   Ervin
at Bo and Luke's 50th Wedding Anniversary Party

Luke & Bo, Cat & Jason, Growing Old

Ode to Luke

To Luke, my love, my husband rare
I offer gratitude and praise.
To what he gives, none can compare - -
He loves me, helps me, cares always.

For fifty-six short, wondrous years
We've walked together, strong and proud.
His strength and comfort allay fears - -
His motives soar above the crowd.

God did, with Luke, my life endow.
Before his life, Gibaltar moves.
His character makes Everest bow.
His steadfast worth, our marriage proves.

Great poets boast of Motherhood
And Brotherhood acclaim.
But Husbandhood's a chosen role
For true, deserved fame.

- - Bo Buice, 1996

Ode to Luke which Bo Wrote to Him in 1996

Ervin Luther Buice (Luke's) last picture, 9-9-01

Bo & Nelle Hayes Arden Reunite after 18 Years

Bo & Nelle in Fairfax, VA on Nov. 7, 2005

Bo Buice, Nelle Arden & Linda Martin

Susan Whitener Gardner, Bo's Cousin 11-10-05

Bo & Linda travel to Washington in 2005 to
visit Nelle Hayes & Susan Whitener Gardner

B2 / Saturday, Nov. 12, 2005   METRO

Photos by JASON GETZ / Staff

Gwinnett County Police accident investigators **S.N. Bozeman** (right) and Sgt. **Wayne Thaxton** examine the Amtrak train that collided Friday in Norcross with a driver who tried to cross the tracks while the crossing arms were down.

Man killed in train crossing crash

By BEN SMITH
bsmith@ajc.com

A man who attempted to drive around lowered railroad crossing arms was killed Friday when his car collided with an Amtrak train, police said.

The 8:30 a.m. collision on Langford Road, just west of Buford Highway, set off an explosion that incinerated the 2004 Kia Amanti and its unidentified driver, said Gwinnett County police Sgt. Wayne Thaxton.

No Amtrak passengers were hurt and the train wasn't seriously damaged, though it was delayed for about three hours, said spokeswoman Tracy Connell.

The speed limit for passenger trains on this stretch of track is 79 mph, police said.

The train tore through the driver's side of the automobile, ripped off the trunk lid and rear fender and sent pieces of the car flying up to 200 yards away.

Near the wreckage lay dozens of fliers for a Duluth shoe repair service and two mismatched boots.

"All we know is that the victim is a small-sized male," Thaxton said at the scene.

As of Friday evening, Gwinnett police hadn't released the victim's name.

Thaxton said the collision occurred when the eastbound driver apparently attempted to the cross the tracks with the barriers down and the warning lights flashing.

Tom des Islets came running outside after he heard a loud thud on the sliding door of the warehouse where he works. He saw the Kia engulfed in flames. Part of it had hit his building, 150 yards from the crash scene.

Des Islets said cars on Langford Road routinely get backed up from Buford Highway past the railroad tracks during rush hour. Des Islets said he's seen drivers get trapped between the crossing bars because they didn't have enough space to clear the tracks.

"I see people get caught on these tracks all the time," he said.

A wrecker hauls off the unidentified driver's 2004 Kia Amanti. The vehicle caught fire after it collided with the train at a crossing on Langford Road.

The 150 passengers on Amtrak's Crescent train waited as Gwinnett police and federal investigators surveyed the damage. None of the passengers were allowed to disembark during the delay.

Thaxton said some of the passengers that he interviewed were unaware that the train had hit anything.

"They described it as a slight jolt," he said.

The New Orleans-bound train was 30 minutes away from its Brookwood Station stop in Atlanta when the collision occurred. Its journey began in New York City.

Article about the train crash on their return trip via Amtrak

Epilogue

We have come to the end of our journey into the life of Bo Buice and her family, her work, her ministry. Lest the reader come to the conclusion that her's was a perfect life, without faults or mishaps, I felt led to say that her's was not. I learned a long time ago never to put any person too high, because all people are imperfect, and they will fall from their pedestal eventually. There was only one perfect Person who ever lived, and His Name is Jesus Christ. All the rest fall short of His glory. He is the only One who deserves to be "worshiped."

Oswald Chambers wrote in his classic devotional, ***"My Utmost for His Highest,"*** " . . . . have I got beyond all confidence in myself and in men and women of God; in books and prayers and ecstasies; and is my confidence place now in God Himself and not His blessings?" We are to worship the Creator, not the creation nor the creatures.

I know this is what Bo would have you take with you at the close of her story, not that she should be put upon a pedestal, as if she were an idol, but that her life should point you to the God whom she loved and served all her days on earth. She wouldn't mind, however, being called a "heroine," a woman of godly character, who inspired you to steadfast endurance and Christlikeness as you live out the remainder of your days on earth.

Bo would have us all look to the Savior, the Author and Finisher of our faith, the One who will see us through until the end, so that we all finish well. He is the Good Shepherd, who looks after His sheep, and calls them each by name, whom we are to emulate, to follow. His are the words which will transform and inspire us to victory. His Spirit will lead us and guide us into all Truth as we seek Him diligently, and put Him first in our lives. He chooses us all, but some "sheep" follow Him more closely than others. These are the ones He can trust, who stay put and don't constantly wander away from the flock. The Lover of Our Souls goes after the "lost" sheep to bring them back. into the fold. There is great rejoicing over the "one" who was lost and is now found. I pray if you are one of those "wandering one's" who has strayed away from the flock that Bo's story will draw you back into the Shepherd's arms of safety and security. "The eternal God is your refuge . . . . and underneath are the everlasting arms." (Deuteronomy 33:27a)

Bo Buice (90) & Nelle Hayes Arden (89) -- Good Friends Until the End

Ervin (Jason), Bo & Luke bid you all farewell

OMEGA—THE END

"Christ died for us; we die to our sin, and we die physically and return to Him—the reality of death. Recently I have been thinking differently about death because they (my loved ones) are there. Losing my family has been extremely difficult. I need Luke, Jason and Cat, but their going has made me look forward to joining them someday in heaven."

"And by the way, I am no saint!"

—Bo Buice

Max Lucado's words on the front of a card to Bo reads, "We don't like to say good-bye to those whom we love. It is right for us to weep, but there is no need for us to despair. They had pain here. They have no pain there. They struggled here. They have no struggles there. You and I might wonder why God took them home. But they don't. They are, at this very moment, at peace in the presence of God."

"The end is actually a brand new beginning for the believer."
—Linda M. Martin
June 1, 2006

H—Holy	B—basic
A—Attitude	I—instructions
P—Praising	B—before
P—Praying	L—leaving
Y—Yielded	E—earth

Relax . . . . God is in control!

BVG